BEST
W~~~~
1960

D1130711

THE FABULOUS
TOBY AND ME

The
FABULOUS
TOBY
AND ME

By
Neil E. Schaffner
with
Vance Johnson

PRENTICE-HALL, INC.
ENGLEWOOD CLIFFS
NEW JERSEY

*To those patrons whose love
and loyalty kept that
bit of Americana called repertoire
alive for so long*

———————

THE FABULOUS TOBY AND ME
by Neil E. Schaffner with Vance Johnson
© 1968 by Neil E. Schaffner and Vance Johnson
Copyright under International and Pan American
Copyright Conventions
Library of Congress Catalog Card Number: 68-13060
Printed in the United States of America
T
Prentice-Hall International, Inc., London
Prentice-Hall of Australia, Pty. Ltd., Sydney
Prentice-Hall of Canada, Ltd., Toronto
Prentice-Hall of India Private Ltd., New Delhi
Prentice-Hall of Japan, Inc., Tokyo

INTRODUCTION

ONCE UPON A WONDERFUL TIME THERE WAS A GREAT AMERICAN institution called tent repertoire. All across the country, traveling companies of actors came to town once a year, erected a huge tent on a vacant lot somewhere and presented "a new and different play each and every night."

You really got your money's worth. Every night there was a free "military band" concert in front of the tent. When the concert ended, you could get inside the tent for a half-dollar or less and take a seat on the circus bleachers at the back. Or, for an additional quarter, you could gain admission to the "reserved seat" section and luxuriate on a soft pine folding chair. Something happened every minute. By the time you got settled, an orchestra took its position on a platform in a corner of the tent, near the stage, and entertained for half an hour. Then the play began, often continuing for four acts. Time between the acts was consumed by vaudeville performances of various kinds and on Saturday nights, and often during the week as well, there was still another performance after the play—a tabloid revue or a fast-stepping vaudeville show. You could see this for another quarter.

If you were lucky enough to live in a place like my hometown in Texas as many as three or four tent shows came every year during the harvest season, and this added to the experience. You could count on two out of every three companies to offer a grand old play like *Lena Rivers* or *Saintly Hypocrites and Honest Sinners*, so you had an opportunity to compare different productions before the performances became misty memories.

The "legitimate" theater looked down its long nose at this kind of entertainment and few indeed were the Broadway actors who would even admit they learned their trade in the tents. But in the decade before the Great Depression tent repertoire (*never* called repertory) not only was the lustiest but the most robust branch of the American theater. Writing for *The New York*

Times in October 1927, Don Carle Gillette, editor of the show business trade paper *Billboard,* declared that "the canvas playhouses of the country now constitute a more extensive business than Broadway and all the rest of the legitimate theater industry put together."

"According to the records kept by *Billboard,*" Gillette wrote, "there are at present approximately 400 tent theater organizations scattered around the United States. Nearly all of them play a season of forty weeks or more. Many run nearer fifty, and some never lay off at all. The shows, for the most part, have a repertoire of six to a dozen bills and it is the usual policy to remain a week in each stand. Consequently, at a conservative estimate, 16,000 communities are served with theatrical performances each year through the medium of the tent shows. The legitimate theater, on the other hand, now has less than 500 houses in the entire country. About 150 of these are in New York, Chicago, Los Angeles, Boston and Philadelphia [and] the actual number now getting Broadway stage attractions is around 300. The tent-drama, therefore, visits 51 places to every one visited by the Broadway drama."

Gillette estimated that tent repertoire gave 96,000 performances a year before 76,800,000 people, compared to 80,000 performances before 48,000,000 people in the legitimate houses.

Tent repertoire had been around a long time before the 1920's. No one really knows where it started but the first successful tent impresario probably was a man named Yankee Robinson, who in the 1850's formed Yankee Robinson's Opera Pavilion and offered a repertoire of "popular dramas and comedies" at Rock Island, Illinois. One of the early touring tent repertoire companies was J. N. Rentfro's Jolly Pathfinders, who were trouping along the Gulf of Mexico by the early 1870's. The Ginnivan Dramatic Company of Indiana began an annual summer tent tour in 1881 and J. C. Rockwell started touring New

England soon thereafter, offering such plays as *The Two Or-phans* with a cast of ten. The Choat Bros. Big Shows, a reper-toire company despite its carnival-sounding name, started in Illinois in the eighties. M. L. Kinsey, manager of an opera house repertoire company in Ohio featuring his wife Beth and their daughter Madge, took his show out under a tent in 1901 and Charles Harrison began touring Texas in 1906.

By the summer of 1916, fifty or more well-known companies were touring "established territories" in the Middle West and elsewhere. Roy E. Fox had joined Rentfro and Harrison in Texas, the Aulger Bros. were in Iowa and Maurice and Ed Dubinsky of Kansas City had four companies on the road—one in Oklahoma and three that divided up portions of Kansas and Nebraska. Jack and Maud Brooks were trouping parts of Illi-nois and Wisconsin and Clyde Gordonier and his brother Earl both had shows in Illinois. Clyde featured comedies and Earl serious drama.

Many of these companies were merely opera house repertoire troupes moved outdoors for the summer season, when most theaters were dark because of the heat. Essentially the same brand of entertainment—drama interspersed with vaudeville—had thrived in theaters across America since before the turn of the century and from 1900 to about 1920 repertoire was Amer-ica's great family theater. The better rep companies charged fifty cents for the orchestra, thirty-five cents for the balcony and a quarter for the gallery, but so many charged a thirty-cent top that "10-20-30 rep" became a generic term. Literally hun-dreds of companies trouped back and forth across the country, playing three-day or week stands in towns large and small, and scores of them played the same towns year after year. In New York, Boston, Chicago, Philadelphia and other large cities, reper-toire thrived in the neighborhoods while the long-run plays and high-priced stock companies occupied the center of attention downtown.

A great change took place after World War I. The moving picture industry, gaining power as its product improved, gobbled up theater buildings everywhere—even buying houses it could not use in order to eliminate live competition—and repertoire moved under canvas wholesale. The tents were much cooler than the theaters in summer and millions of people still preferred the spoken play to the flickering images projected silently on a silver screen. Almost any kind of dramatic company could make money under a tent, and there were all kinds. William and Nora Leonard, traveling out of Ridgeway, Missouri, mixed circus and repertoire—giving a circus performance in the afternoon and drama at night—and the Walter Savage Company in Nebraska combined a carnival and a dramatic show. Rides and concessions operated before and after the play. Many small family shows, with four or five people and a piano, thrived in crossroad hamlets but many more large companies, with elaborate tent theaters, toured the Middle West, the South and Southwest. Thirty or more performers, actors, musicians and vaudevillians, were not uncommon and many of the companies offered one or more recent Broadway hits on every repertoire. George Sweet's Famous Players, who toured northeastern Iowa, offered New York releases exclusively. *The Family Upstairs*, *The Gorilla*, *The Noose* and *Lightnin'* all were great successes in the tents.

Early "canvas playhouses" were circus tents—large ovals designed for arraying the audience around one or more performing rings in the center. Being of the theater, the pioneer tent "repsters," as *Billboard* called them, naturally put the stage at one end of the big tent, ranged circus bleachers, or "blues," across the back and sometimes down the sides as well, and placed wooden chairs in the center in the manner of the ordinary theater. This arrangement had one very serious drawback: a large pole was required to hold up the tent at the stage end and this rested immediately in front of and at the center of the stage.

But about 1920, a man in Kansas City invented a new "dramatic end" tent which eliminated the bothersome center pole and tent showmen at last were able to match the large city theaters in production, with fine lighting and effects, elaborate sets and frequent changes of scenery.

For at least one glorious season The Paul English Players, who toured the South from Louisiana to Virginia and billed themselves as "The Show with a Million Friends," carried a veneer front containing a thousand electric lights and at each stand they actually dug a pit for the orchestra. A hydraulic device lifted the musicians to the stage level for their feature numbers. Charles Harrison trouped with a tent theater so large and elaborate that he required three days for the set up at each stand and a day and night for teardown. He carried complete flat scenery for each play, portable houses for dressing rooms and a floor for the tent, to which seats were attached in the manner of a permanent theater. Horace Murphy's show in California had a huge revolving stage and in Texas, Harley Sadler's tent had a regular theater fly loft for the scenery and a proscenium arch a hundred feet across. Most tent theaters had a simple, if colorful, canvas marquee in front but in Iowa, the Hazel Cass No. 1 show had a regular theater lobby, with the box office on a raised platform. Miss Cass also employed a maid in the ladies' dressing room.

Many accomplished actors preferred the steady work of tent rep to the uncertainties of Broadway, and on the better shows directors demanded highly polished performances. Pearle Wilson, who spent thirty years in tent rep, said she felt "terribly let down" when she finally got to New York.

"I went to *Harvey* and *Oklahoma!*, among others," she said. "The way some of the minor roles were played was a disgrace to the profession, and a good tent show never would have permitted lighting like they had in *Oklahoma!*, where the actors threw shadows on the backdrop, which was a field of grain."

Pearle Wilson can be pardoned a rather rosy memory of rep;

primarily she worked shows like Murphy's Comedians, Harley Sadler & His Own Company and The Schaffner Players of Iowa. Too many tent shows, alas, were shoddy affairs, with diamond-dye sets, actors of questionable ability and an eye for a quick buck rather than customer satisfaction. When hard times hit after 1930, these shows quickly disappeared from the scene. The better companies kept operating for a time, but with the Great Depression there also came the talking picture and, soon thereafter, air conditioning. People with money to spend—and there were all too few of them—naturally preferred the upholstered seats of an air-cooled theater to folding wooden chairs in a tent on a sweltering summer night. One by one the tent shows dropped by the wayside. Those that the Depression did not get, World War II did.

One kept right on going, year after year: The Schaffner Players. There were two excellent reasons for this: Neil and Caroline Schaffner. Imaginative, resourceful, tenacious—and, above all, performers of great virtuosity—they somehow managed to turn every tragedy into a triumph. They survived the Depression and two wars and did their biggest business after television aerials sprouted on rooftops all over their territory. Time came when they could work twenty weeks a year and bask in the Florida sun the rest of the time.

The Schaffners' success was compounded of many things, but the solid base was Toby. In a real sense, Toby was Neil Schaffner and, as you will see, Neil Schaffner was Toby.

VANCE JOHNSON

CONTENTS

The stories here recounted have been told and retold by me so many times over the last half century that I believe them myself. I hope they are as true as I think they are.

Neil E. Schaffner

PART ONE

Rehearsal

Rehearsal

1

TOBY WAS A RUBE IN THE GRAND TRADITION. HIS HAIR HAD A sheared-on-the-farm look. He usually wore overalls and these likely as not were held up by one gallus. He spoke a barnyard brand of English and many of the more cultivated customs of society were beyond his ken. Yet underneath Toby's country appearance and unsophisticated manner there ran deep currents of native wit, of cunning and resourcefulness. Unlike many of the rubes before him, Toby was True Blue. Sometimes he actually rose to the heroic, though invariably he made it appear accidental.

Like Topsy, Toby just sort of grew. It was like this . . .

In the summer of 1911, an actor named W. C. Herman wrote a new play and broke it in on the C. Carleton Guy Repertoire Company, a tent show in Indiana. Public reaction apparently was indifferent because Herman later completely rewrote the script and titled it *Clouds and Sunshine*. He sold it outright to Alex Byers, a play broker in Chicago, for one hundred dollars. In 1912 Byers sent a copy of the script to Lorin H. Guin, the director of a popular price resident stock company at the Magic Theater in Fort Dodge, Iowa, my hometown. I was the juvenile light comedian in that company and it happened that just a few days before Guin received the Herman script he and I had been talking about the sad state of repertoire comedy.

"What I can't understand," I said, "is why so much comedy has to be based on ridicule—why the comic character so often is more to be laughed at than with. If he's a Swede, he's always dumb and if he's a Jew he's an unethical skinflint. If he's black-face he's ignorant, superstitious and shiftless, and if he's a rube he's just plain silly. It's all derogatory."

Among the rube characters I had done on tour were Hi Holler in *Way Down East* and Jim in *My Jim*. Hi was something like the Mortimer Snerd character that Edgar Bergen created many years later—stupid but likeable. Jim was more of a lead than a comedy character but he was an engaging fellow and audiences seemed to like him.

"I wish somebody would write a play that had a comedy part combining the best qualities of both of them," I said.

"So do I," said Guin. "Some day ethnic groups are going to resent the kind of humor we have now and boycott it."

The discussion ended on that prophetic note. One afternoon after rehearsal, several days later, Guin asked me to drop by his room at the Crawford Hotel.

"I've got a script with a character in it something like the one you were talking about," he said. "If you like it, we'll put it up."

Clouds and Sunshine was just another church play, a form that was very popular at the time, dealing with the exposure of small town religiosity and hypocrisy. The part that caught Lorin Guin's fancy, Tobe Haxton, was a minor part. Tobe did nothing to advance the plot; he and a schoolgirl named Susie Green just wandered on and off stage, making wisecracks and in a shy way burlesquing the love affair between the principals. But there was something warm and human about Tobe and I was drawn to him at once. We went into rehearsal the next day.

Herman described Tobe as "a young fellow about eighteen or twenty, not particularly bright but good-natured—the village errand boy." The script called for Tobe to dress in "overalls, boots and a slouch or straw hat," but I thought he ought to have something more distinguishing about him. Rummaging through my trunk for wardrobe, I came across a red wig that I had bought for an Irish character and had worn with a sort of beard that ran from the temples around the chin. By itself, the wig resembled a very shaggy, uncut head of hair and I thought it would be just about right for Tobe. To complement the wig, I put on a ruddy complexion and some big blotches of freckles, then arched my eyebrows a bit to produce a pixie effect. As an afterthought, I slightly turned up the corners of my mouth. The result was just what I hoped for; on my first entrance, before I had opened my mouth, a titter of laughter swept across the theater.

In Tobe's first scene the leading man, Reverend Joe Tucker, inquires solicitously about Tobe's father and Tobe quickly reminds him that the man he calls Paw, who is a drunkard and an ornery one at that, is not really his father but just "a man Maw married" after his real father died. During the course of the conversation Tobe casually asks if he can borrow some horse liniment and ultimately the minister's housekeeper appears with a bottle. Reverend Tucker asks what Tobe is going to do with it.

> TOBE: I'm goin' to give it to Paw.
> TUCKER: Why, Tobe, it will kill him!
> TOBE: Sure?

That surprising twist got a huge laugh and there was at least one good belly shaker every time Tobe was on. In one scene Samantha, the housekeeper, complains to Tobe about something the Reverend Tucker has done and asks, "Why didn't he tell me?"

> TOBE: Well, maybe he didn't think it was any of your business.
> SAMANTHA: What the minister does is *everybody's* business.
> TOBE: Well, when he gets ready for everybody to know it, he'll tell you.

All through the play, whenever anyone does something displeasing to Tobe he says, "Next time he does that, I'll whale him with a whiffletree." Each threat is more ludicrous than the one before it and although we gave only three evening performances and one matinee of *Clouds and Sunshine*, "I'll whale him with a whiffletree" became a standard gag around town.

The week following our brief run, Guin wrote Alex Byers about how *Clouds and Sunshine* had been received in Fort Dodge and commented at some length on my characterization of Tobe Haxton. Byers then sent the script, together with Guin's testimonial, to Horace Murphy, who then had two repertoire companies playing in tents in Louisiana under the name of Murphy's Comedians. Murphy sent it over to his No. 2 unit where a young, redheaded actor named Fred Wilson was the comedian. Wilson liked the play and introduced it in the middle of one week's repertoire. The reaction was so favorable that he opened with it in the next town.

The second bill on that week's repertoire was *Won by Waiting*, in which the comedy character is named Bud. Before Bud's first entrance he is mentioned several times and finally the character woman goes to the door and shouts, "Bud! Bud! You come right in here!" When Wilson hit the door a small boy down front called out, "Heck, that ain't Bud! That's To-be!"

On sudden inspiration, Wilson stepped out of character and advanced to the footlights to address the boy.

"You're right, son," he said. "I *am* Tobe and from now on everybody is going to call me that."

Wilson's instinctive response to that boy set off a chain reaction that swept through the whole repertoire business. Horace Murphy visited the No. 2 unit several days later and when Wilson recounted his experience he immediately decided that from then on all rube characters in plays presented by Murphy's Comedians would be called Tobe. Both shows had a tremendous summer and Fred Wilson became so popular that even on the street people began hailing him as Tobe. Before long he was billing himself as Tobe Wilson and the name stuck for the rest of his career.

Word of such success naturally spread through the business and within a year rep plays with comedy characters remarkably like Tobe Haxton turned up all over. Some ingenious playwright, plagued by conscience if not by the copyright laws, changed the spelling from Tobe to Toby and that stuck. Scores of uncelebrated playwrights adopted Toby as their own. Some endowed him with more wisdom or cleverness than others and some saw in him only a buffoon. But all of them portrayed him as a brash or upstarty or sly farmhand, or cowboy or town "character," with an uncanny ability to bumble into and out of comic situations.

Dozens of comedians shamelessly stole the main elements of other actors' characterizations of Toby, even to makeup. Every one of them wore a red wig, sprinkled his face with freckles and peaked his eyebrows. Many gave him outlandish wardrobes from time to time but none kept him out of overalls for long and, whatever he wore, he practically never was without a bandanna. Some played Toby broadly, some sympathetically, some tastefully and some crudely, but if you saw one actor's Toby you were prepared for the next one who came along. The better Tobies became so identified with the part that in the public mind they lost their own identities. Across my old territory in Iowa more people still greet me as Toby than as Neil.

Millions of showgoers paid cash admissions to see Toby. Yet, so far as I know, all that Cal Herman ever got out of Tobe Haxton was the hundred dollars that Alex Byers paid him for the original script.

2

I did not play a Toby part again for several years and it was a long time before I became a Toby comedian. But when the time came we were ready for one another, Toby and me, and looking back after a half century it does not seem strange at all.

My grandfather, John H. Schaffner, owned gambling and liquor concessions on steamboats plying the Mississippi River in the 1840's. In Fort Dodge, where he settled in 1855, he ran one of the town's more elegant saloons as an adjunct to the Wahkonsa Hotel, which he owned. To his premature death at forty-nine, Grandfather's everyday dress included a velvet coat and a velvet vest with gold pieces for buttons. The coat buttons were twenty-dollar-pieces and those on the vest were five-dollar-pieces. He would have felt right at home among the rep actors I knew in my youth.

Then there was my Dad, whose name also was John H. He was a little fellow with a bony face and a pronounced hawk nose —made that way, he said, so he could hang by it and pick cherries with both hands. Everybody around Fort Dodge called him Johnny and that was what he was: just Johnny. It was not that Dad lacked industry or anything like that; he just dreamed a lot. When I was a small boy he always was talking about looking up an old Indian friend of Grandfather's over around Dubuque. When Grandfather moved his family from Dubuque to Fort Dodge, Dad, who was nine years old at the time, rode the whole distance atop a chest which he said contained fifty thousand dollars in gold. He was convinced that Grandfather had buried a like amount of gold somewhere around Dubuque and that the old Indian would know where it was. He never did get back to Dubuque, though.

When I was a small boy Dad made a living mostly by sign

painting, house painting and paperhanging, but his big failing
was that he did not know how to adequately charge for his work.
Often when he had completed a time-consuming, artistic sign
he would only charge a couple of dollars for it, though even in
those times it was worth several times that. For several years he
also worked as a car finisher in the Illinois Central Railroad
shops, varnishing and striping the ornate wooden interiors of
passenger cars. Even when he was eighty years old, he could
take a striping brush and draw a line so straight you would think
it had been printed by a printing press.

Dad had three avocations: acting, painting and growing
flowers. He took part in a great many amateur theatricals in
Fort Dodge and was an end man in the annual minstrel show for
several years running. He loved everything about show business
and one of his dreams was to travel in advance of a show, painting original billboards instead of hanging printed paper. Though
it still is a mystery to me how he ever had the time for it, Dad
painted a great many pictures, most of them landscapes. I have
three of them hanging in my home. His work was much admired
around town and he and Grant Wood, a much younger man,
became good friends. Once when Wood had a showing of his
paintings in the window of one of the big stores on Main Street,
he insisted on showing one of Dad's canvases along with his. Dad
painted numerous murals in restaurants and bars around Fort
Dodge, for inadequate pay, but if he ever sold one of his paintings I never knew of it.

Growing flowers was something else again; Dad could make
anything grow. When I was a small boy I helped him sell flowers
from a booth during our annual street fair and he eventually
went into partnership with two other men, built several green-
houses and did well as a florist.

Dad was one of seventeen children and I was the last of five
boys and three girls. He was a widower and Mother was a
widow when they married. Mother had two girls and Dad had

two boys by their first marriages and their union produced three sons—Rome, Frank and me—and a daughter who died in infancy. Frank, who was seven years older than me, also became an actor. He took Francis Lacour as his stage name and for some reason never altogether clear to me, everyone in the business called him Jap. His career spanned more than forty years and at the time of his death in the early forties he was free-lancing as a radio actor in Chicago.

Mother shared Dad's love of the theater and they were such regulars at the Old Fessler Opera House, which for a long time was Fort Dodge's only theater, that all of the actors called them Mom and Pop. I was just five years old when they took me to see my first play. I think it was *Muldoon's Picnic*.

When time came for it to start, a man dressed as a butler came out from behind the curtain and lighted the kerosene footlights. He was joined by a woman dressed as a maid and they carried on a considerable amount of conversation about the play. When the curtain finally did go up the play went on for four or five acts, with interminable intermissions for changes of scenery, and then when that was over the company put on another very funny little one-act play. The idea, I suppose, was to leave them laughing. I was completely transported by the whole affair. To me, the people on the stage were not merely actors but the people they represented, caught up in the very situations they portrayed. I had an almost overpowering desire to get up behind the footlights with them—a sensation I experienced every time I went back to the Fessler, which was often.

By the time I was ten years old I was a confirmed playgoer and in that year, 1902, a wonderful thing happened in Fort Dodge: the new Midland Theater opened. It was simply splendorous. The orchestra was on the ground level, not upstairs over a store like the Fessler. To get to it you walked through a lobby which seemed immense to me, past a box office with a grilled window. Seats throughout were regular theater seats, with curved bottoms and backs, not straight chairs and gallery benches like the Fessler's. There were two balconies and, for the benefit of those who came to be seen more than to see the show, four boxes. The stage was enormous: about fifty feet deep and a hundred feet wide. Two huge metal doors opened directly onto the alley and one day a man drove a two-horse beer wagon through them and circled the stage just to see if it could be done. Scenery was of the latest box type, not the Fessler's old grooved type (which fitted into grooves in the ceiling), and the drops and curtains "flew" into a vast fly loft above the stage. The first man responsible for this department was a fellow named Hopper, who sometimes hit the bottle a little hard. Hopper worked from a bridge about thirty-five feet above the stage and one night during the run of the original *Sis Hopkins* show, when he had had a few too many, he went to sleep and fell off the bridge. Fortunately, the most important prop on stage at that moment was a big hayrack and Hopper landed in it.

The house manager at the Midland was an industrious fellow named Bill Dermer, who during the day clerked in Joseph Hyman's clothing store. He also had a number of sidelines, among them posting billboards and distributing advertising handbills around town. He did most of his bill posting at night, pushing his materials around in a handcart lighted by a very uncertain gasoline torch that at times flared up so high it seemed to me it would consume cart, billboards, Dermer and all, then died down until Bill almost disappeared from view. Dermer was a big man but he was so dextrous with his long-handled posting brush that I loved to watch him and followed him around whenever I could. Ultimately, Bill hired me to pass out handbills—my pay being a seat in the gallery at the Midland. Then, when I got a little bigger, he gave me a job carrying out ashes at the Midland and I was so diligent at that that he let me employ two assistants.

Then all I had to do for my admission was to tell them where to pile it.

For a while I sold peanuts and chewing gum at the Midland on commission for Roy Stevens, who ran a store on Main Street, and from that I graduated to the theater checkroom. These jobs required my presence at the theater every night and so I got to see just about every kind of theater entertainment.

Fort Dodge was then a city of about twenty-one thousand (under Iowa law then a town could have one saloon for each one thousand inhabitants and Fort Dodge had twenty-one) and thus attracted many companies that played the larger cities. All of the more famous midwestern repertoire companies played the Midland, among them North Bros., for whom Warner Baxter was leading man several years later, the Dougherty Bros., Flora De Voss, and Frank E. Long. One company which always did big business was the Irving E. French Company, which had a very unusual advertising policy. French's billboards usually contained just three lines:

IRVING E. FRENCH COMPANY

Opera House

SEPTEMBER 12

One year, though, French plastered the town with paper for *Finnegan's Alley* as if he intended to play only a one-night stand, when as a matter of fact he was booked for three nights. *Finnegan's Alley* was an extremely popular play and on opening night he had a packed house. Before the first curtain, French came out and gave some reason why the play could not be presented that night, but assured the audience that if they came back the next night they would see it. The substitute play was well done, with a lot of fancy dress, and so he had a big house the next night. True to his promise, French did present *Fin-*

negan's Alley, but before the last act he announced that on the third and final night of the company's stay he would give away a diamond ring "absolutely free" to the patron whose lucky ticket was drawn. The ring was not worth much more than the price of admission but he packed the house a third time.

Many stars of the day came to Fort Dodge every year, each time in a new play. Among these was William B. Patton, who billed himself as "the peculiar comedian." Patton spoke in a very slow, deliberate drawl and in one of his big hits, *The Slow Poke*, a characteristic gag was: "What's th' use o' runnin' when there's plenty o' time to walk?" He was a sort of poor man's Sol Smith Russell but he had a tremendous following. Bob and Eva Mc-Ginley also had an unusual show for those times. They put on the entire play themselves, doubling in parts and making quick changes. They apparently played all over the Middle West because later, when I got into the business, I found little advertising stickers with their names on them in dozens of opera house dressing rooms. They did skip at least one. In a small town in North Dakota some actor had scrawled in crayon on the back of the opera house curtain, "Bob and Eva ain't been here yet."

Extremely elaborate productions were commonplace at the Midland. The *Ben Hur* company carried eight horses, four chariots and a huge treadmill on which the horses raced. Lincoln J. Carter's immortal melodrama, *The Flaming Arrow*, carried a number of real Indians and at least one horse, a beautiful buckskin ridden by White Eagle, and there was another show that had an exciting scene in which a jackknife bridge opened and a man on a motorcycle raced up and jumped five or six feet across the opening. The *Span of Life* show had a strange setting that included two high cliffs with a chasm in between. In one scene three acrobats made a human bridge across the chasm—the bottom man's feet resting on one cliff and the top man's hands grasping the other. At a climactic moment, the heroine raced across on their backs and when she was safely across, the bottom man let go and they all clambered up the other side and fled offstage.

I made my first stage appearance in one of these spectacular shows, *The Devil's Auction*. Among other things, the show had a number of acrobats who played the parts of imps, and a comedy character called Toby (no relation to Tobe Haxton). One set had a number of trapdoors in the flats which were disguised as paintings on a wall and every once in a while an imp would race across the stage and dive right through a picture. Then there was a hilarious scene in which Toby walked into a cabinet on one side of the stage. As the door closed behind him several of the imps jumped on top of the cabinet, causing it to telescope. Then the imps opened the door and a flattened-down Toby stepped out. That was me. My costume was a replica of Toby's, padded all around to give the illusion of having been flattened, and this was topped with a papier-mâché head and face. All I did was step quickly into the cabinet as Toby made a hurried exit from a trapdoor at the back, then let somebody take me by the hand and lead me off the stage, but it got a big laugh and that, for me, was heady stuff.

Another one-nighter, *Lover's Lane*, came to the Midland and my cousin, Dick Colby, and I got to do a fight in a school-yard scene. *Lover's Lane* came back the next year and as soon as we got wind of its coming, Dick and I practiced our fight scene for several weeks. When the company arrived we presented ourselves to the manager and told him we were familiar with the important fight scene and rehearsed. He said we were too big and gave the job to two rank non-professionals.

In summer, when the Midland was closed, Fort Dodge usually could count on two or three of the more famous one-night stand tent shows to come to town. Dr. Rucker's Korac Wonder Company, a medicine show which presented drama instead of circus and vaudeville acts, also came one summer and stayed for several weeks, putting on a different three-act play each night. Before the last act, Doc Rucker came out and said his company could play any drama ever written and asked for requests for the following night. There's an old story, not hard to believe, about one such request for *Trilby*. Doc is supposed to have called the company together and asked, "Any of you birds ever played *Trilby?*" None of them had.

"Nevertheless," Doc said, "tomorrow night we play *Trilby* and the first sonofabitch that calls her Kathleen is fired."

He was referring, of course, to *Kathleen Mavourneen,* a grand old repertoire bill that every rep actor and most audiences knew.

3

The beginning of the twentieth century was a great time for being a boy and I cannot imagine a better place to have been one than Fort Dodge.

Fort Dodge straddled several hills that looked down on the Des Moines River and whoever selected the site must have had boys in mind. It was a great place for sledding in winter, especially Pottery Hill. If you had a good bobsled you could start at the top, about Fourth Street, and go almost straight down for about four blocks, then level out and scoot almost to the Rock Island Station on Soldier Creek. With all the creeks and other places among the hills where water stood and froze over, there was good skating almost all winter. And in summer a fisherman could find almost any kind of action he wanted. There was a place above town where Lizard Creek emptied into the Des Moines River that nearly always yielded catfish and carp and once in a while a pickerel or a bass. Up Lizard Creek a ways there was a good spot for bass and channel cat, and another place just above the Bobtown Bridge over the Des Moines was good for redhorse suckers.

There never was much money around the Schaffner house for

the more important boyhood luxuries, like Flexible Flyers or split bamboo casting rods or skates with shoes attached, but I managed. Mr. Twigg, the blacksmith who lived across the alley from us, bolted my old clamp-on skates to an extra pair of shoes and also built a wonderful sled for me. It had steel runners which were fastened to two-by-six boards and because of its weight it could outrun practically every other sled in town. For bobsledding, another boy and I pooled our resources by linking our two sleds together with a board and connecting the front sled to it with a bolt so that it could be steered. I made my first casting rod myself from the small end of an ordinary bamboo pole. My total investment was a nickel for the pole and a nickel for some copper wire to make the guides. Until I acquired enough cash to buy regular hooks and lines I made hooks out of some of Mother's darning needles and used some carpet thread for a line. And one summer I made a canoe, using some one-by-two boards for the keel, barrel hoops for the frame and some old canvas for the cover. Since our house was twelve blocks uphill from the river, I used some baby buggy wheels and an axle to make a dolly for transporting the canoe back and forth.

One of my boyhood pals, Glen Churchill, lived in a room over Olson's Drug Store and he and I whiled away many rainy summer days there reading Balzac's *Droll Stories* and books like that, giggling over the racier passages. Dave Hyman and I also spent a lot of time in the public library. There always was something worthwhile to do—like shagging free rides on the new Fort Dodge streetcars, or setting off skyrockets at the top of the hill at Twelfth Street and watching them go screaming down the tracks almost to the park down by the river. Or lying under the railroad bridge over Soldier Creek and looking up between the ties as the girls picked their way across, giggling and pretending embarrassment. Or shooting rats off the rafters in the loft of the livery barn with my .22 Hamilton single shot, or slipping into the ball park through the uncovered men's toilet in the right-field corner to see Fort Dodge's Iowa League team. Or riding up and down North Ninth Street on a bike in the evening when the new asphalt paving—the first smooth paving in town—was completed.

One summer, when I was about ten, I organized my own baseball team—being the pitcher, of course—and also worked very hard on an act I was sure would make me a big-name circus performer. The feature attraction at our street fair that summer was a Japanese wire-walker named Prince Uturki. He worked on a wire strung across the street from the tops of two buildings and I was so impressed I tried to duplicate his act, practicing on a wire which I stretched between a telephone pole and a shed in our backyard. I did very well, too; before the summer was over I could prance back and forth with the aid of a balancing pole like Uturki's, lie prone and do various other impressive stunts. But then school started and the Midland reopened and my attention was directed to other things.

Another summer Dick Colby and I organized our own theatrical company, which we called The Park Theater, for no reason except we liked the sound of it. Above Mr. Twigg's blacksmith shop was a kind of hall that was not being used for anything and we made arrangements through Dick's grandfather, who owned the building, to use that for our hall. We built seats and a stage out of some old boards placed over empty beer kegs that we got from the back of the Moist Goods Saloon, which was owned by Dick's father, and we fashioned the wings and backdrop for the stage out of some cast-off wallpaper. This done, of course we needed a vehicle and I provided that because I was already pretty experienced at playwriting. For quite some time I had been dramatizing parts of the Horatio Alger books and acting them out in the privacy of my room.

The play bore a striking resemblance to *The Royal Slave*, which the George H. Bubb Company had brought to the Midland the winter before, but I called it *The Last of the Monte-*

zumas. I can remember only one line from it, in which Father
Aguila, "an Indian priest," says, "Dare you, beneath the shadow
of the cross, do the work of the devil!" I took the part of Father
Aguila, of course, and with Mother's help fashioned a costume
out of some long-handled underwear, dyed red, some beads and
turkey feathers. I have forgotten what part Dick played and I
cannot remember any girls in the cast, though I know the script
called for certain female characters.

Dick had a Pony named Sparkle and a little surrey with a
fringe on top. To advertise our production, I put on my Indian
costume and as we drove up and down the streets I touted the
show, shouting through a megaphone. We charged ten cents
and the show probably was worth it. We opened to capacity
business and though we put on the play only spasmodically,
when we needed a little money I guess, it seems to me now that
we always played to a pretty good house. Most of our auditors
were kids, but now and then we attracted a few adults from
among our relatives as well.

Around that same time somebody in Fort Dodge put on an
amateur vaudeville show and Dick worked up a patter and gag
act for it with another boy. I hung around all the time when
they were rehearsing, and my disappointment at not being included in the act must have been pretty apparent because Dick
finally worked me into it. I was blacked up and when he and
his partner went on stage I went on, too, put down a bucket
upside down, and sat on it. When they were through, I picked
up my bucket and walked off stage with them.

"Neil," Dad asked me that night, "why didn't you at least
kick over that pail?"

4

In 1905, when I was thirteen, Bill Dermer made me the assistant property man at the Midland and a whole new world
opened up for me.

Backstage they talked a language I had never heard before.
The men who moved the scenery about were called *grips*, the
fellow in the catwalk above the stage was the *flyman* and the
man in charge of everything, strangely, was called the *stage
carpenter*. When a scene in a play took place in a living room,
the thing we put on the floor was not a rug but a *medallion* and
the piece of canvas under that was called the *ground cloth*. The
horizontal masking that stretched across the proscenium arch,
hiding the upraised flys from the audience, was the *grand drapery*
and in the center of that there was an extra piece that could be
raised or lowered for various purposes and this was the *teaser*.
The vertical scenery pieces on either side of the stage were
tormentors. The four basic sets were *front room, back room,
timber* and *town*. The *town* set consisted mainly of a drop showing a street scene; *timber* was a woodland setting and *back room*
was a plain chamber that usually served for a kitchen set. *Front
room* really was two sets. One represented a parlor in an ordinary home and the other, known as *center door fancy*, represented a rich man's drawing room. The fancy had an arch up
center, a door right and a door left and it practically always
contained a table and two chairs right and a settee left. Some
radical directors changed things around and put the table and
chairs left and the settee right, and some even went so far as to
put the settee center, flanked by the armchairs.

All this stage-hand jargon, though, was elementary compared
to the language spoken by the actors. An actor never played a
part, he *did* it; he never traveled, he *trouped;* he never appeared

in a play, he *worked* in it. The thing he memorized was the play; the thing he performed in was a *bill,* and the individual pages in his part were *sides.* When he knew his part he was *up in it* but when he blew his lines he was *up.* When an actor's dressing room was a long way from the stage, he complained about his *sleeper jump* and if a show failed he said it *soured.* Bad towns were referred to either as *bloomers* or *lemons.* I later played both Bloomer, Wisconsin, and Lemon, South Dakota, but I do not remember whether they qualified or not.

Men who specialized in robust, two-fisted, he-man parts were referred to as *blue shirt leads* and many of them actually did wear a blue flannel shirt. Women who played little girl and late teen-age parts were referred to as *soubrettes* (the term ingenue did not come into general use until much later) and those who specialized in hillbilly or rural girl parts were known as *rough soubrettes.* The good guys in the white hats made so popular on television, incidentally, were nothing new; in 1905 women who played mean parts always wore black wigs and the heroines wore blonde wigs.

The standard cast for repertoire companies was "four and three"—four men and three women. These usually included a leading man, a light comedian, a character or heavy man, and a general business man, a leading lady, soubrette and character woman. Some of the better companies carried as many as five or six men—the extras being "general business," meaning they could play whatever was required. Extra women were called "second business" and usually were cast as female heavies though, when required, they also did the soubrettes.

Actors never were out of work, they were *at liberty,* and when caught in this situation they usually passed their time backstage with working actors. They always were welcome but if there was anything actors, at liberty or not, could not abide it was a towner who claimed to have been an actor but never was. There were all kinds of tricks for unmasking such characters, but a favorite stunt was to ask casually what the visitor had done in *East Lynne*.

There's a scene in *East Lynne* in which Richard Hare is asked what he has been doing and he replies, "I've been working in the stable yard." A favorite piece of business, which very few directors would tolerate, was to emphasize the line by scraping the feet backward, so if when asked what he had done in *East Lynne* the visitor immediately scraped his feet he was accepted as a professional.

I don't know why they went to all that trouble because you could pick a rep actor of that day out of any crowd. Nearly all of them wore either Ascot or Windsor ties and distinguishing Stetson hats with broad, flat, stiff brims. In winter nearly all of them wore Paddock overcoats, which had flared-out skirts and either velvet or fur collars. Managers and many leading men wore diamond rings and stickpins and carried gold-headed canes, and managers' wives always wore fur coats and as many diamonds as they could keep out of hock.

In my newly-found eminence as assistant property man, I was accepted on some level of near equality—much nearer equality, I was to find out, than I would enjoy as a budding actor—and I hung around the actors every minute I could, soaking up their manner of speech and listening to their boasts. I watched them make up and dress for the show and when a show ended its run I went through the dressing rooms collecting tubes of makeup and anything else they left behind.

Around 1905 there were two main lines of theatrical makeup, Hess's and J. F. Warnesson's. The Hess line was available in most drugstores and thus was used by amateurs, but Warnesson's could be secured only by direct order from Chicago. It was looked upon by professionals as a sort of status symbol. Warnesson's came in tin tubes and all those left behind at the Midland, naturally, were practically empty. I heated them on Mother's cook stove to melt the remaining greasepaint, then mixed the paints together as required to produce filled, professional-looking tubes for my own use. Late at night I sat before the dresser in my room and practiced making up, and while many of my colors resembled nothing human, I thought I did a pretty good job of making myself look old or like an Indian or anything else I fancied.

Altogether, I worked most of three seasons backstage at the Midland, graduating from assistant to property man the second year. (For this I got not only fifty cents a performance, which was fifty cents more than I had received as assistant, but also a pad of complimentary passes to distribute around town in return for borrowed props.) During this time I met several celebrities of the day, one of them being Frank James, who came to Fort Dodge with a road show called *The James Boys of Missouri*. Frank had just been pardoned from the Missouri penitentiary. He was a soft-spoken, kindly old man with a snowy white beard and it was terribly hard for me to think of him as a notorious outlaw and killer. I also got to meet Jim Jeffries and Gentleman Jim Corbett, the great heavyweight prizefighters.

Jeffries, who was a simply horrible actor, was starring in a play which had a setting in the north woods and in one scene a girl was in a cabin surrounded by howling wolves. Finally she cried out in anguish, "Will nothing save me?"—and at that point Jeffries materialized from somewhere, advanced on the door and thrust a powerful arm through some large leather loops that apparently were designed to hold an iron bar. "Yes," he said flatly, "the strong arm of a backwoodsman."

Actors in those days, incidentally, did not believe in leaving much to an audience's imagination. One very popular play was *At Piney Ridge*. The star, David Higgins, made his first entrance on a *run* (a platform built behind scenic rocks to give the illusion of coming downhill). Before he came on a voice in the distance called, "Jack Rose of Piney Ridge is coming... Jack Rose of

Piney Ridge is coming!" The line was repeated several times and then Higgins loped down the run, hit the stage in a spot and proclaimed, "Jack Rose of Piney Ridge is heah!"

Gentleman Jim Corbett came to the Midland in a show called *Facing the Music*. My brother Jap was in the cast and I spent quite a lot of time in the dressing room with them. One day Corbett got to talking about his father. When Jim came back to Boston after his first professional tour as a boxer with a carnival athletic show he was flat broke. His father sadly shook his head and said, "There's an old and true saying, me by, that a rolling stone gathers no moss." But after Jim had fought his way to the heavyweight championship of the world his father greeted him joyfully. "There's an old and true saying, me by," he said, "that 'tis the roving bee that gathers the honey."

Meeting such celebrated figures was as exciting for me as it would have been for any other boy of thirteen or fourteen, but my biggest thrill came when Charles B. Hanford, the renowned Shakespearean actor, came to the Midland in 1905 in a repertoire of three or four plays. Since David Hyman's father had the complete works of William Shakespeare in his library, I had read every one of the bard's plays by the time I was thirteen—some of them several times. I memorized long passages which I acted out before the mirror in my room. One afternoon during Hanford's stay in Fort Dodge, I stole into the great man's dressing room and, standing before his makeup table, began to recite a passage from *Richard III*, which was my favorite among Shakespeare's plays.

> Now is the winter of our discontent
> Made glorious by this summer sun of York,
> And all the clouds that hovered o'er our house
> Are bro'en and gone

Just then, in the mirror, I caught the sight of Charles B. Hanford himself, standing in the doorway. I was thunderstruck. I blushed. My mouth flew open and I just stood there, mute, for an eternity. Mr. Hanford smiled warmly. At last I found my tongue and apologized as best I could for uttering such a parody of one of his great speeches and finally managed to say, "Some day, sir, I hope to be a great Shakespearean actor too."

"I hope you will, my boy," he said, putting an arm around my shoulder and giving me a little hug, "I surely do."

5

In the fall of 1907, while still working as property man at the Midland, I landed a very minor part in a production of the Fort Dodge Dramatic Club called *My Partner*. We gave several performances in Fort Dodge and then went up to Humboldt for a one-night stand and after that I knew that work backstage was not for me. I wanted a job *on* the stage. Where? That was the question, but independent vaudeville looked like a possibility.

A number of movie houses not big enough to get on one of the established vaudeville circuits had begun to book free-lance vaudeville acts as extra attractions, so I decided to make my availability known to them. I had a letterhead printed with a picture of me in a flat-brimmed hat and a line identifying me as *The Original Silly Kid* and parted my name in the middle: N. Edward Schaffner. I wrote to several houses and in a fairly short time landed a date in Estherville. When I got there the house manager informed me that they changed bills in the middle of the week and that he expected me to do an entirely different act on the second half. I assured him I had plenty of material and I really thought I did, but when I went out for my first turn I used everything I had in five or six minutes. I lasted only to the midweek change.

Returning to Fort Dodge, I teamed up with another stage-struck boy, Bill Beaver, in a new act. We called ourselves McNutt and Morley. We had letterheads printed and bought some large photographs of ourselves for display on lobby boards in the theaters we expected to play. To make sure that we had plenty of material, we sent off to one of the play publishing houses for a little two-man sketch called *Is He In?* It ran about fifteen minutes and contained such brilliant passages as this:

> MCNUTT — Is he in?
> MORLEY — Is who in?
> MCNUTT — The man I came to see.
> MORLEY — Who do you want to see?
> MCNUTT — The man I'm looking for.

We also worked in *Bit from Nature, Entitled Little Tim,* a recitation that Mother loved to have me give for visitors in our home. It told the story of a wharf rat, "nabbed" for swimming "in the city front" but saved from jail when a rich man pays his fine, although demanding to be repaid in a year. It concluded with these dramatic lines:

> Well, nigh a year had passed when Tim and me was sneakin' another dip when a steamer run too hard agin the ferry slip.
>
> A little kid was sittin' on her daddy's knee and was knocked clean over the side of the ship.
>
> We looked and saw it was the same rich bloke. Then in like a duck dove Little Tim.
>
> Oh God! that kid could swim!
>
> When he came to the top he had the kid by her long yellow hair. When they pulled 'em up on the deck the kid was all safe and sound but Tim, poor little Tim, was hit by the steamer's wheel. In his side was one big wound.
>
> The daddy knelt and kissed his kid and then looked to where Tim lay, so cold and sick, and said, "God bless you kid." And Tim looked up, his eyes wet with tears and said, "I can't pay you all, mister, I'm four bits shy."

Bill and I booked several dates but I soon had an opportunity to do a single as an "announcer" at the Delight Theater, a new movie house in Fort Dodge, and withdrew from the act. At the Delight I stood on a platform to one side of the screen and described the action as it unfolded, calling attention to the more subtle aspects of the picture, like this:

> See, now this girl is going into the store. She's coming out, and notice she has her handbag in her hand. Now this man approaching her is a masher and he's going to try to make a hit with her. See! He tips his hat....

During the long lapses between reels of the movie, when the projectionist was rewinding film, I also sang illustrated songs: "Won't You Come Over to My House and Play?" "It's the Man in the Overalls" and other fine ballads of the day. As I sang, magic lantern slides illustrating the songs were flashed on the screen.

I had been announcing for several weeks when Mr. Spencer, the manager of the Delight, offered me a new job: advance agent for a feature picture he had acquired and wanted to send on tour in other towns. I was expected to make deals with the local picture houses for showing it on a percentage basis, pass out handbills, tack posters on telephone poles and otherwise advertise the show. The first town was Manson, about twenty miles west of Fort Dodge, and after I had made all the necessary business arrangements I started out to put up my advertising. I walked up to a telephone pole and raised my hammer, and that was the last I knew until I woke up at home in bed two or three days later. I had smallpox.

To avoid having the whole family quarantined, Dad fixed up a bed for me in the shed on the back of our lot and I spent twenty-one lonely, miserable days there. About the only thing that made my incarceration tolerable was the supply of cigars that my brother-in-law, Bill Ehlerding, brought me. I do not really remember when I started smoking. Like other boys, I had smoked tea and coffee, buggy whip, corn silk and anything else that would burn during my earlier youth, but for some time before my fifteenth birthday, thanks to Bill, I had been smoking tobacco exclusively. Bill ran a cigar factory in Fort Dodge and in return for my help in stripping tobacco leaves kept me well supplied. He was especially thoughtful while I was laid up with smallpox, making my cigars entirely from binder, the expensive leaf that was used to enclose the filler core of cigars before the outside layer was applied.

While I was recovering, a new company was formed in Fort Dodge called Talking Motion Pictures—Ta-mo-pic for short. Their scheme was to have live actors recite the lines as the play unfolded on the screen and another fellow and I and Dick Colby's sister, Florence, landed the talking parts. We sat behind the screen at a small table, with a shaded lamp in front of us, and read all of the parts from a script provided by the makers of the picture. We did three shows, *East Lynne*, *Lady Audley's Secret* and *Romeo and Juliet*, but unfortunately Ta-mo-pic's bookings lasted only a few weeks. I returned to Fort Dodge and started answering ads in the New York *Clipper*.

The *Clipper* was the leading theatrical paper of the day and since actors at the Midland often left copies in their dressing rooms when they departed I had been an inveterate reader for a couple of years. Every issue carried advertisements listing openings in repertoire companies. Most of the ads specified "band actors" or "actors doubling bands" and some went so far as to say "every man must double B. & O. or B. & S."—meaning the actors had to work either band or orchestra and musicians had to carry parts. Since I played no instrument this left me out, but occasionally there was an opening for an actor who had a line of vaudeville specialties and could take on some other job in the company. I answered all of these. Whatever they wanted, juvenile, leading man, character man or what have you, I was it. At last, just before my sixteenth birthday, an ad finally appeared that exactly fitted my qualifications: Maxam & Sights Comedians needed a man to handle props, play small parts and do specialties. My letter drew an immediate response from J. W. Sights, the manager. He offered me "five dollars and cakes" and directed me to join at Walker, Minnesota.

Dad loaned me money for my railroad fare and I reached Walker on a Sunday afternoon. On Monday night Jim Sights told me that among my other duties I was to handle the curtain. This pleased me very much because I always had admired how Swifty Atkins brought the big curtain down at the Midland back in Fort Dodge and I had vowed that if ever I got the chance I would make her thud just like he did. The opening play in Walker was *East Lynne*, which ends on a very pathetic note as the dying Lady Isabel says to Archibald, "Farewell, farewell Archibald, until eternity." As she expires, Archibald folds Lady Isabel's arms across her bosom, looks heavenward and says, "Till eternity." The opera house in Walker had a roll curtain and when Archibald finished his line I let her drop. The curtain hit the stage with a loud crack and bounced a foot in the air. I thought I had really done something until I glanced up and saw Mr. Sights. He nearly turned purple.

The next night I went out for the first time to do my Silly Kid routine between acts and nearly fainted when I discovered that the first several rows were filled with Indians. I had never seen any real live Indians before except on the stage and I'm sure my apprehension was apparent as I started my monologue:

> I'm not feeling so good, I just got out of the hospital. Had
> my vermacella asparagus cut out.

I paused for laughter but those bronze faces just stared up at me.

> They cut me open from the meduval to the longata to the
> thorax, then all points south on the Santa Fe.

The Indians apparently had never heard of the Santa Fe.

> All I remember is when they put me in there and laid me on the table I heard one feller say to the other feller, "Shall we give him ether?" "What's that fer?" one feller says, and the other feller says, "So he won't know nothing." And then the first feller says, "Well, that won't be necessary in this case."

There was not even a snicker.

> Anyway, I remember when I woke up I was in a room and the blinds was all down and I yelled at the doctor, "Hey doc! Whoa, doc! Come here! What's the idea of them blinds being down?" He says, "Well, young man, there was a fire raging across the street and we didn't want you to wake up and think your operation had been a failure."

I heard a few uncertain laughs toward the back of the house but those Indians did not laugh or smile or even act as if they had heard me. I tried another joke or two and these went over like lead kites, too, and when I left the stage I was sure that I somehow had offended the Indians and dire retribution awaited me after the show. But when the final curtain fell the Indians got up and left with everybody else, and just as silently.

Maxam & Sights had some strong vaudeville but it was not a very good show. Jim and Paulina Sights both were in their fifties but Paulina nevertheless played the ingenues and Jim, a very portly, most unromantic man, played the leads. We limped along for just three weeks, then closed at Black Duck, a little Minnesota mining town near the Canadian border. I had only enough money to buy a railroad ticket to St. Paul. I was walking around the depot there, trying to figure out how to get the rest of the way home without wiring Dad for money, when I happened to see a familiar face behind the ticket window. It was Mark somebody who had been ticket agent in Fort Dodge and when I told him about my predicament he gave me a ticket. So, as the saying goes, I came back home on the cushions.

I went back to high school in September but was bored miserably, so I kept answering ads in the *Clipper*. Finally, in late April or early May 1909, I got another reply—this time from Sam Spedden, manager of the famous Spedden & Paige Dramatic Company, then preparing for its annual tour of Minnesota and adjoining states. The job, like the one with Maxam & Sights, was to handle props, do minor parts and specialties, but Spedden offered "fifteen dollars and pay your own." At seventeen, and near the end of my sophomore year in high school, I decided that I had had enough formal education for an actor.

For the next several days I scurried about, rounding out my wardrobe. Before leaving Fort Dodge I had acquired all of the essentials:

> Broad-brimmed hat
> English walking suit with a round-cut coat reaching almost
>   to the knees
> Prince Albert coat with satin lapels
> Windsor tie
> Formal dress outfit
> Western outfit, complete with chaps, spurs and leather
>   wristlets
> Satin square cut, with lace foils in the sleeves and a lace
>   collar, knee britches and white hose for French costume
>   dramas
> Oil cloth boot tops, worn over regular shoes to look like
>   miners' boots

At the last minute I acquired the most important of all my equipment: a flat-top Taylor trunk. This was an absolutely essential badge of professionalism; in fact, many actors thought it was bad luck to have anything but a Taylor in the theater. Al Butters, the manager of the Crawford Hotel, had taken a Taylor in settlement of some actor's bill and gave it to me. Dad painted

"Neil E. Schaffner, THEATER" on the top in large, ornate letters. Thus equipped, I dispatched a telegram to Mr. Spedden
requesting an advance to pay expenses in joining—this being a
sure sign that I was a professional. He wired me ten dollars.

The train ride from Fort Dodge took all day Saturday, Saturday night and half of Sunday. After paying my fare, there was
only enough money left to buy some Sweet Caporal cigarettes
and a few candy bars, but as the train pulled into Aberdeen I
do not recall the slightest feeling of hunger. As soon as the brake-
man put his step down and got out of the way I rushed forward
to oversee the unloading of my Taylor trunk and strolled along
as the baggage man wheeled it to the depot, confident that the
connection did not go unnoticed. Crossing the street to the Commercial Hotel, I registered, signing Spedden & Paige boldly behind my name where my address should have been, and at once
set out to meet my new employer, who was stopping at another
hotel. On the way I circled the block several times to admire
the Gottshaulk Theater, where we were to appear, and each
time tarried long enough for the Sunday strollers to take notice
of my Windsor tie and flat-brimmed Stetson. At that moment
I would not have traded places with the President of the United
States.

When I entered his room, Sam Spedden was sitting before a
window in his undershirt, reading a newspaper, but when he
arose I sensed why he billed himself "King of the Northwest."
He was tall, extremely handsome and very dignified. Beside him
his wife, Claire Paige, was tiny. She was a strikingly good-looking woman with natural red hair. Both greeted me warmly and
seemed to take such genuine interest in my trip up from Fort
Dodge that in no time I was calling him Sam. But when I called
her Claire, the climate suddenly changed. She icily informed me
that her name was Mrs. Spedden.

Being anxious to let him know I had one, I asked Sam who

would take care of my trunk and he referred me to Harry Manners, who was staying at the same hotel. Manners was the stage manager and director of Spedden & Paige and, like Sam, was tall and good-looking. The resemblance ended there. He accepted my trunk check without comment and all I got out of him was the bare minimum of information about the schedule for the forthcoming week. As I prepared to leave he took a typewritten part from the top of his dresser and handed it to me.

"Our opening bill is *The Woman in Black*," he said. "Have you worked in it?"

"No," I replied casually, "that's one bill I've missed."

6

First rehearsal was at ten o'clock Monday morning but I got to the theater at nine. My trunk was in a corner of the stage among many others but the name did not show so I turned it around. Then for nearly an hour I walked back and forth across the empty stage, reciting lines from every play I could remember, and feeling terribly important.

Shortly before ten the other actors began to arrive and although there were some perfunctory introductions no one seemed overcome by my presence. Harry Manners appeared at the stroke of the hour and rehearsal began. My part was a light comedy, the son of a wealthy man, and in the play I was supposed to be about two-thirds drunk in the first scene, staggering on after singing a little song offstage. When my cue came I sang my song and walked on. In those days actors never acted at rehearsal, they merely recited lines, and I had seen enough rehearsals at the Midland to know that.

"Now cross down left to the end of the settee," Manners directed. I did that and said my next line.

"Now cross over right," he said, and I did that.

"Did you mark it?" he asked.

"What?"

"Did you mark your part?"

I looked at him rather helplessly and said no.

"Don't you have a pencil?"

"No."

"Young man," Manners said, "you can't sneak into show business."

But sneak in I did. In spite of the large number of companies then on the road there were surprisingly few repertoire plays and most experienced rep actors were up in almost any bill a manager decided to put up. As Manners handed me each part he inquired whether I had worked in it.

"No . . . no," I replied, "I've never worked in this particular play."

During the first week we got up in six plays and when he handed me the last of them, Harry said, "You know, Neil, I've been trying all week to find *some* play you've worked in."

At long last we came to opening night. I took my place in the dressing room next to Willard Collins, the character man, and started making up as if I had been doing it for years. As I leaned back to admire the result Collins wryly observed, "You've got on a false face." I had given myself a peaches-and-cream complexion down to my chin but had neglected my neck. I hurriedly finished the job.

My first scene required full dress and I felt elegant as I took my place outside the center door. There, for the first time, I put on my top hat, which an actor at the Midland had given me. To my horror it was about four sizes too big. Then came my cue. There was nothing to do but pretend to take it off as I entered, and carry it around throughout the scene, crown up. As the scene ended there was a piece of stage business in which I bumped into a doorjamb, backed up and staggered out on the second try. This got a laugh and pleased me very much, but Sam Spedden was waiting for me just outside the door.

"Speak up, young man," he said. "Speak up! I can't even hear you here in the wings."

After the play, in my nervousness, I left some of the makeup on my neck. Next morning I put on the same collar (all dress shirts had detachable collars then) and as I was entering the theater for rehearsal a small boy stopped me.

"Hey, mister," he asked, "where do you fellers git them collars with the pink edges?"

At last, I had arrived as an actor.

While performing the first six plays on the repertoire we got up in six more and rehearsed each of them twice. Minor as my parts were, many of them had long and highly involved speeches but somehow I managed to learn them all—and verbatim. That was the way they had to be learned if you stayed on the show.

Throughout the two weeks in Aberdeen, Sam Spedden remained entirely unruffled and amiable toward me and all the rest of the company. He left the whip-cracking to Harry Manners. In the weeks that followed, however, I learned firsthand that under the amiability there lay a character of steel. Sam was a perfectionist. During performances he moved constantly around the set, checking on the smallest details and giving directions from the wings if the action faltered. To assure quality production, he carried so much scenery, both flats and hanging stuff, and so many props and effects that a forty-foot baggage car was required to transport them.

Among my many and varied responsibilities, I found, was installing and operating the scenic and sound effects. Sam had devices that produced the sound of wind and thunder, rain and snow and almost any sound that a play required. When he did not have one he demanded that we make it on the spot. A big attraction at fairs and other events on the Northern Plains during the summer of 1909 was a dirigible, which a man operated by walking back and forth on an open catwalk suspended beneath the gas-filled balloon. Sam worked a reference to the dirigible into one of the plays and was not satisfied until I created offstage an acceptable sound of the dirigible's motor. (A piece of leather attached to the guard of an electric fan so that it barely touched the revolving blades did it.) In another play he demanded a half-moon that glided slowly across the sky as the story developed. I managed that with a pasteboard box with a moon cutout and a ten-watt light bulb. The cutout was covered with pale green celluloid and when the box, mounted on a wire in the flys, was pulled slowly across stage behind a blue diamond-dye drop, it looked surprisingly real.

One of our rigs produced an effect that you often see these days on television. A comedy character would take a drink of whiskey and spit it toward the footlights; when it hit there would be a big puff of smoke. This was achieved by attaching an electric light circuit to two nails on a pine board, stretching an exposed wire between the nails and covering it with black powder. At the climactic moment, the current was switched on, the wire got hot and the powder exploded. Rheostats had not yet come into use for dimming lights but we achieved this by plunging two sticks of carbon, attached to the electric light circuit, into a keg of water. When the sticks were pulled apart slowly, the water created resistance and the lights dimmed; when they were moved back together the lights brightened. The same device was used to create offstage lightning; when the carbon sticks were pulled apart abruptly a sharp flash of light resulted. It was as dangerous as all get out, but effective.

Sam surrounded himself and Claire with an extraordinarily capable and versatile cast. The most colorful was Bill Collins, a distinguished-looking middle-aged man with a voice almost musical in its wide range of qualities. Bill had an amazing wardrobe. It included something with real character in it for every part: old, rundown-at-the-heels boots, threadbare and dirty old clothes, red undershirts, beat-up old hats and what have you. Of course he had all of the other essentials, too, and when a part called for it he could be impeccable on stage, though I never understood how. On opening night in every town, Bill pulled a table over beside his trunk and as the engagement progressed he lifted clothes out of the trunk, wore them and then piled them on the table. On closing night he just swept the whole pile off into the trunk, stuffed it down and closed the lid, yet when the clothes came out in the next town they looked as if they had been freshly pressed.

Altogether, there were fifteen people in the company: thirteen actors, a piano player and an advance agent. All of the actors had between-acts specialties and two of them were as fine as I ever saw in big-time vaudeville—an act by Louella Montague, Harry Manners's wife, working domestic cats and white rats in the manner of circus lions and tigers, and one in which Larry Wilson tossed hoops about the stage in such a manner that they did intricate maneuvers in returning to him. None of the actors doubled in brass. Music was provided by local house musicians or, where there were none, by the piano player.

7

The 1909 Spedden & Paige routing included towns large and small, but most of them were small. From Aberdeen we worked our way down to Sioux Falls for a two-week stand, then played week stands in one hamlet after another until we reached Deadwood. So far as I am concerned, that is where the West began.

Deadwood's main street was about four dusty blocks long, three of them made up of saloons, gambling establishments and houses of ill fame. There were two honky-tonks, the Green Front and the Bodega, much the livelier of the two being the

Bodega. It was like today's nightclubs, having tables over the main floor and a stage at one end. There was one main difference: around the outer walls it had private boxes with curtains that could be drawn when privacy was desired. The Bodega girls worked in the chorus, hustled drinks and other things and were dressed in very daring costumes. When they kicked you could see an expanse of bare thigh. One of the girls sang a very racy song ending with the line: "Her name was Mary Wood but Mary wouldn't." The most surprising thing about the show was that a man singer, not the girls, always got the biggest hand from the crowd of drunken miners, cowboys and whatnot.

After Deadwood we played Belle Fourche, South Dakota, and then jumped by horse-drawn stagecoach to Sundance, Wyoming, three stages being required to haul the company. The only place for me was on top of the lead stage beside the driver—the seat that "Shotgun" always occupies in the westerns. When we were passing through the Black Hills the driver suddenly drew his six-shooter and killed a rattlesnake that was sunning itself on a rock. He did not even slow down.

"Boy! That's some shooting!" I exclaimed.

"Naw, that ain't shootin'," he said. "A rattlesnake'll always strike at a bullet."

Several people later solemnly assured me this is true but I don't vouch for it.

Sundance was a town of about three hundred people. It had no newspaper or telegraph but it did have an opera house seating about two hundred and it was packed every night. Admission was a silver dollar. People were so glad to see us that we were guests of the town all week. We could pay for nothing, not even our hotel bill; when we left by stage for Gillette the proprietor of the hotel put a large hamper of food and a case of beer in each coach.

In Gillette I met three young men who were said to be professional gunslingers. They certainly looked the part but they were so agreeable that I enjoyed their company very much.

They called themselves Pants, Marion and Doc. One night toward the end of the week they took me with them after the show to a back room in a saloon, where a number of tough-looking characters were waiting. After the door closed behind us, Pants informed me I was to be inducted as an honorary member of the Walla Wallas, which he said was a secret society that was very strong all over the West. The most important thing I learned about the Walla Wallas was that if lonely or in need I always could flush out another Walla Walla, by carefully following their recognition ritual. In such cases, my instructor told me, I was to place my right hand on my right lapel as I walked down the street and if another Walla Walla was present he would come up to me and we would exchange greetings as follows:

"Where you from?"

"Back east."

"Where you going?"

"Out west to grow up with the country."

"Would you take money from a woman?"

"Every cent."

"Would you give her any money?"

"Not a dime."

"Are you a Walla Walla?"

"I am."

"Then duke me, kid."

I never did learn what the Walla Wallas were for. It could have been just a great big joke among people who traveled from town to town but I did try out the ritual several times and a Walla Walla always was present. I hope they don't come gunning for me for giving away their secrets.

After Gillette we played Buffalo, which intrigued me because it was the locale of Owen Wister's story *The Virginian*. The corral where Trampas was supposed to have taken a shot at the Virginian was still standing. From there we made an historic trip to Sheridan—the inaugural trip of "the first motorized stagecoach in America," a seven-passenger white Steamer touring car. Sheridan was memorable for me because it was there I had my first drink of whiskey.

At Cheyenne, which we played during rodeo week, I got acquainted with a bronc rider who called himself Montana Jack. He had a beautiful pair of boots, with his name woven into the design on the tops, and I admired them beyond words. On our last day in Cheyenne a man appeared at my room in the hotel bearing them. He handed me a crudely written little note from Montana, saying he hoped I would wear his boots on the stage. I never saw or heard of Montana Jack again but I did, indeed, wear those boots on the stage for many years.

Most of the so-called opera houses were just bare rooms, usually over a store, with flat floors and tiny stages rarely high enough to accommodate our scenery. The opera house manager invariably earned his living at something else and never was on hand when we arrived so I would chase all over town until I could catch up with him and get a key to the place. Nearly always, the preceding event at the opera house was a dance, and it fell to me to put all the chairs in place and find someone to help me move the piano down off the stage. Most of the houses had kerosene lights. When we got ready to start the show we had to wait for the janitor to come slowly down the aisle, pulling the lamps down from the ceiling with a chain and turning the wicks down. For footlights, most of them had lanterns strung across the front of the stage but in one house there was an ingenious arrangement which lowered the lamps below the stage level, and out of view of the audience, for a reasonably satisfactory dimming effect. In another, all of the footlights were attached to a long rod which, when moved backward or forward, lowered or raised the wicks. In the few places that had electric lights, there never were any bulbs in the sockets when we arrived. I would have to chase down the manager a second time to get them, and then only about half of them would burn.

Nearly all of the actors carried a "grouch bag," a little chamois
bag which they wore around their necks, and most of them de-
nied themselves many things until they had a hundred dollars
gold in it for get-home money. I had one made, too, in a saddle
shop somewhere along the way but I found so many interesting
things to spend my wages on that my get-home cache was pretty
slim. Toward the end of the summer this inspired Ed Tierney,
the advance agent, to a poem.

> The prop man sat in lonesome land
>   With the fringe on his pants and his head in his hand.
> As he sat there with eyes downcast
>   He wondered how long the show would last.
>
> Why shouldn't it last? Thus did he muse
>   As he sorrowfully gazed at his soleless shoes.
> With plenty of paper and me in the cast,
>   Even with a bum agent it ought to last.
>
> Oh what is that they call? Oh let me see!
>   It must be good news—oh tell it to me!
> The show closes next Saturday. Golly gee,
>   How far is it to Fort Dodge? Twenty three.

Ed's poem was prophetic. Up on the Northern Plains, where
snow became so deep during winter that people could not get to
town, theaters operated in the summer instead of winter, as in
Fort Dodge. Spedden & Paige usually began their tour about the
first of May and closed a while before or after Thanksgiving,
depending on the weather. The late fall of 1909 proved to
be unseasonably mild and to stretch the season as long as possible Sam booked a number of one-night stands of *DuBarry*, our
feature play, into December. By a fortunate set of circumstances
I got to play the important Richelieu part. Harry Manners, who
had played Richelieu all summer, left the show when he and
Louella separated (they later were divorced) and Sam gave me

the part. I already was up in it; in fact, I knew every part in
every play on the rep.

DuBarry was a very elaborate, richly costumed play and the
part of Richelieu was simply tremendous. In the first act, I made
a dramatic entrance down a staircase, interceded in a sword fight
between two soldiers and after much clashing of steel put them
under arrest. This done, I had a long soliloquy, lasting three or
four typewritten pages. I was on the stage a big part of the first
and second acts and in the third act I had a very dramatic scene
with Claire Paige, who was DuBarry. The king is dying of the
plague and has left orders that DuBarry is not to be allowed into
his bedroom. She is on her knees, begging Richelieu to let her in,
and Richelieu says:

> The end of Louis XIV merely marks the end of one
> reign and the beginning of another. When the end has
> come, when the king is dead, the cannons in the citadel
> will boom and the cathedral chimes will toll the mournful
> message to Paris and to France. . . .

At that point I decided to take a dramatic pause—to act a little
—but Claire, who was hard of hearing, misunderstood. When
she saw my lips stop moving she thought I was up and started
ad-libbing to get me back on the track. I squeezed her hand,
trying to let her know I was all right, but she apparently thought
I was flirting with her or something because she just squeezed
my hand right back. I finally stepped around so that I could
look her right in the eye and continued, as loudly as I could
shout:

> . . . The passing of Louis XIV is neither the beginning
> nor the end of Richelieu's power . . . and Richelieu is your
> friend!

The audience must have thought we were nuts.

We did very well with *DuBarry* for a while, but then we got
to Hot Springs, South Dakota, and a strange thing happened.
Most actors are superstitious. Yellow is considered a bad luck

color; it is bad luck to whistle in the dressing room, to put a shoe on a makeup shelf or a hat on a hotel bed, or to use a Bible on stage (a dictionary always is used instead). And in those days it was considered bad luck to speak the last line of a play in rehearsal (the actor would just say "tag"), but the illest omen of all was the playing of "Home Sweet Home" in the theater. That meant the show would close for sure. In the early evening before our appearance in Hot Springs, several of us were in the dressing room when we heard someone out front playing "Home Sweet Home" on the piano. We all rushed out on the stage and as we got there an elderly man was just finishing the chorus. He arose and walked out of the theater, not saying a word.

None of us had ever seen him before and never saw him again, but business was lousy that night and after two or three more nights of disappointing audiences the notice went up and we closed for the season.

I worked for Spedden & Paige four straight summers, spending the off season in Fort Dodge and occasionally doing an independent vaudeville date or working as a motion picture operator. During those four years I had watched Cecil Manners, Harry's daughter, grow up from a cute little kid into a petite, very pretty and vivacious young lady. During the summer of 1912, when she was sixteen and I was twenty, we fell in love. Cecil's mother, Louella Montague, tried to discourage our romance but late in the summer she learned that she had to have a goiter operation at the end of the season. She was scared to death and began to worry about what would happen to Cecil if she did not survive the operation. Finally, she gave her permission and Cecil and I were married when the show closed, around Thanksgiving. I took Cecil to Fort Dodge to meet my family.

When my father met her he turned to me and said, "You could have got a full-sized one for the same price."

PART TWO

Half Hour

Half Hour

————————— ◄◆► —————————

1

The theatrical situation in Fort Dodge had changed considerably while I was off trouping with Spedden & Paige. The Midland Theater had burned down and there no longer was a house devoted exclusively to repertoire and touring one-price dramatic companies. The Princess, which had become the quality house, booked a dramatic show on occasion but specialized mainly in vaudeville. There also was another theater, the Magic, which for some time had been presenting five acts of vaudeville with movies but in 1912 it was so over-shadowed by the Princess that the owners decided to make it a family stock house, presenting two plays a week at popular prices. When I reached Fort Dodge the Magic was organizing its acting company and I went down at once to inquire whether they could use a juvenile light comedian or, better still, a team. I got a frigid reception.

"We are using New York and Chicago actors exclusively," said the manager, H. Dudley Nashold. "We are not interested in home talent."

A few days later, however, Mr. Nashold called me at home and asked me to drop by his office. An awkward situation had developed. The Magic's grand opening under the new stock policy was only two or three days away and their New York juvenile had not worked out. There was not time to bring on a replacement and Mr. Nashold offered me the job.

"Now mind you," he said, "this is strictly temporary—for the opening bill only. Just this one play."

In other words, I was hired for three days' work, plus a couple of days of rehearsal without pay, and no future. But, being flexible, I accepted and Mr. Nashold at once took me back to the stage and introduced me to the director, Lorin H. Guin.

Guin was a portly, nearly bald man in his early forties with large, round eyes and a rich, resonant voice. He greeted me pleasantly, introduced me to the cast, handed me a part and got right to work. The opening bill was *The Man From Home* and the part that fell to me was the kind of juvenile comedy I had been playing for two summers with Spedden & Paige and, to be honest, the fact that I was a hometown boy did not hurt either. I stole the show from the leading man. The second play was *The Havoc*. The actor Mr. Nashold expected to take over for that bill did not show up so he hired me temporarily once more. *The Havoc* was a short cast play—only three main parts and a bit —and that gave me opportunity to shine again because I was cast as a sort of juvenile heavy and I had done several of those parts, too, on Spedden & Paige. Mr. Nashold gave me a contract for the rest of the season at twenty dollars a week.

I would not advise any bridegroom to take a job like that. With two plays a week to do, we spent practically every waking moment in the theater—rehearsing the upcoming play morning and afternoon and performing the current one in the evening. Often we rehearsed Sundays as well and my young bride was left to while away most of her hours alone. Looking back now, though, I cannot say that this caused me any particular concern for a whole new world was opening up for me through Lorin Guin.

Guin's real name was Guin Lorin Harriman. His father was president of the Iowa Mutual Tornado Insurance Association in Des Moines and his mother, whose last name was Guin, had been a well-known actress in Boston stock before her marriage. The Harrimans were divorced when Guin was a small boy and he spent his formative years first with one parent and then the other, and their sharply different influences warred within him. His father, J. B. Harriman, was the conventional hardheaded businessman who looked upon acting as utter frivolity, but the theater was the center of Mrs. Harriman's universe. When Guin was with her they often were in the company of actors and in attendance at the theater. Although he inherited a strong vein of his father's practicality, the maternal legacy—the artistic temperament and the instinct for exhibitionism—proved dominant as Guin approached manhood. During high school in Des Moines he took part in various school and other amateur theatricals and on graduation, much against his father's wishes, he set out to become an actor. Perhaps through his mother's intervention, he started at the top: as leading man opposite Grace Hayward on tour in her play *Graustark*, and also on tour in the sequel play, *Beverly of Graustark*. Then he landed the part of a colonel on tour with the original *Under Southern Skies* company. One evening during a performance he tripped on the stage and broke a bone in a foot. Thereafter he could not walk without limping and, thinking his days in the theater at an end, he went back to Des Moines to become an insurance man. But he could not get the theater out of his mind.

In 1909, when Elbert & Getchel opened the Princess Theater in Des Moines and established their Incomparable Princess Players company—a group which, incidentally, produced Conrad Nagel, Fay Bainter and a number of others who became famous on Broadway—Guin began taking occasional acting parts again. He also became friendly with H. Dudley Nashold, who then was the manager of one of the other theaters in Des Moines. When the owners of the Magic Theater in Fort Dodge decided to convert it from a vaudeville to a family stock house they persuaded

Nashold to take over the management. He took Guin along to organize and direct the company.

Inevitably, I found myself comparing Lorin Guin and Harry Manners. Superficially they were very different. Manners was very dignified, almost austere, and kept his actors at arm's length; Guin was as approachable as an old friend. Every piece of Manners's direction was an edict; Guin kindly asked, "Don't you think it might help if we worked on it this way?" Underneath, the two men were much alike. In 1909 the dramatic gesture and the sonorous tone were in acting style; in 1912 it had become fashionable for actors to sing their lines. But both Manners and Guin taught a more natural style of acting—both being far ahead of their times—and both were perfectionists. They demanded much from their actors and got it.

Discovering my earnestness about the theater, Guin spent much time with me, coaching quietly during rehearsals and lecturing me in long sessions at night after the show. Over and over he said to me, "Neil, don't think rep"—meaning, think bigger. Many repertoire actors of that time were very stereotyped. If they played an Englishman in one play they forever after played every Englishman in exactly the same manner. Guin kept drilling into me the idea that every character was different and required individual treatment. Early in the season he put up *Teddy O'Malley, Our Irish-American Cousin,* the story of a young Irishman who comes to the United States to visit relatives who have been there for several generations. The part of O'Malley, which I drew, has lots of good comedy and at our first rehearsal I thought I acquitted myself creditably in it. I was especially proud of my Irish dialect, which I had copied from Jerry O'Donald, an Irish immigrant who lived across the street from my folks. After rehearsal Guin and I went to lunch together and we were hardly seated before he burst my little bubble.

"Neil," he said, "let's do a little dissecting of this character you're doing."

"What is it that I didn't do right?" I asked.

"Nothing particular," he replied, "except that you are playing it as if the boy came from Sligo, which is a coast town up in the north of Ireland. Most of the people there speak in a guttural tone, deep in their throats, and I imagine you are mimicking someone who came from there. But the people of Sligo are a rather dour lot—not a joyous group as a whole. O'Malley is just the opposite—a cheerful, bouncy type. While there's nothing in the script that says where he came from, I rather imagine a buoyant fellow like him would have come from Killarney. The people around there are happy and lighthearted and have a high, lilting tone to their speech."

He demonstrated what he meant as he talked and I immediately recognized the striking difference in the dialects.

"How many people in the audience would know that?" I asked.

"Well, maybe none," he said, "but there might be one and if there is, that's the one I want to hit."

Guin was forever creating images of people in his mind. In the restaurant between rehearsals or after the show, he liked to play a game in which he speculated on the backgrounds of complete strangers as they entered. He would point out little mannerisms, habits of dress and grooming and the like that revealed the kind of people they were and the surroundings from which they might have come. This probably was mainly for my instruction because when he handed me a new part he always urged me to study it carefully before memorizing the lines.

"Try to analyze it, Neil," he would say. "Try to visualize the character you are going to do. What kind of a fellow is he? What is his educational background? Is he loud and boisterous or is he quiet and reserved? What is his general attitude toward life? Try to visualize a human being and see if you can fit this character into that mold."

Even in such purely theatrical crafts as makeup, Guin looked far below the surface. When I did my first character part at the Magic I put a lot of dark lines across my face to simulate wrinkles, as many rep actors did, but Guin said, "Let's take it off." He took some dark makeup and deepened my cheeks and the side of my nose, then highlighted my cheekbones. When he finished I looked fifty years older.

"You see, Neil," he said, "in age, the bones stand up and the other parts of the face sink."

We did a western play in which I was a cowboy. In the inevitable barroom fight, I was knocked out. When the man I was fighting hit me on the chin I fell backward and lay still until the curtain came down. Afterward as we were walking to the restaurant across the street for our customary supper, Guin said, "Oh, Neil, there's something I want to tell you: in that fight scene you fell backward."

"Sure," I said. "He hit me and knocked me over."

"You were knocked out," Guin said. "When a man is knocked out he always falls forward."

I do not know whether that invariably is true but every prizefighter I ever saw who was knocked cold by a single punch did fall on his face, not on his back.

In one play there was an angry exchange between two of the characters, one saying something derogatory about the other. Guin was playing the character who was the butt of the remark. Instead of responding immediately he paused, looked away, then slowly looked back before speaking. The rejoinder was of no great importance but the way he paused and turned and then turned back made it sound very profound. After the performance I remarked on how impressive that piece of business was.

"Neil, that's what I mean by the rhythm we have talked about," Guin said. "There is rhythm in acting just as there is rhythm in music. It's knowing when to blurt out a rejoinder and when not to. It's knowing when to come in when the laugh dies, and when to build it more. No one can teach it to you. You have to learn it by doing it, by practicing until it becomes second nature for you to do it right."

I learned more about my trade from Lorin Guin, I think, than from any other man. I learned by soaking up everything I saw him do and practicing it, and I also got a liberal education just listening to him talk.

2

Business at the Magic began to taper off after two or three months and the show closed in April 1913. By that time Harry Manners, who now was my father-in-law, was directing at the College Theater in Chicago for T. C. Gleason. They had just finished a successful run of Cosmo Hamilton's play, *The Blindness of Virtue*, which previously had had a long run in London, and Gleason was forming a road company to take it on tour. Manners got the juvenile lead for me and the ingenue part for Cecil. We went into Chicago to rehearse and then played one-night stands until about the first of July. In time we reached Fort Dodge and the Princess Theater. When the house manager, George Gillman, learned that I was playing a major part he nearly had a tizzy. *The Blindness of Virtue* commanded a two-dollar top and Gillman understandably doubted whether his patrons would pay that much to see an actor they had watched a few weeks earlier for thirty-five cents. At curtain time I was assailed by doubts, too. Standing in the wings waiting for my first cue I felt myself getting weaker and weaker.

I was playing Archibald Graham, Jr., which is practically the star part in the play. In the opening scenes the other characters talk about little else except this boy Archibald, so his first entrance is one of the high points. When the great moment came and I hit the center door, with the stage empty, and looked out front and saw all the leading lights of Fort Dodge in the audience, I suffered the only real case of stage fright in my career. But the audience saved me. They gave me an ovation and by the time it ended I had recovered.

When we closed with that show, Cecil and I once more went back to Fort Dodge, arriving just as a man named Claude Corey was putting together a stock company for a new airdome theater. This was an open-air affair, built like a baseball park, with a stage in the grandstand corner, bleacher seats around the outside fence and folding chairs on the ground in between. Airdomes had become popular for summer theater all over the Middle West beginning about 1910 and by the summer of 1913 nearly every town had one. They did enormous business until 1915, when the entire Midwest had a very wet summer; then most of them went broke and few came back. After that, tent repertoire pretty much took over the summer business.

Claude Corey had a spot only for a single and I probably would have been wise to wait for something else to come along, as it always had. Cecil and I had not enjoyed perfect bliss for some time and while I was working for Corey she got a crush on another actor. We were divorced, but in the fall I landed jobs for both of us on the John G. Rae show, a six-people tank town one-nighter, and we got married again.

Rae was touring with a sorry play called *Her Son* but he somehow managed to stay out until late spring. Cecil and I slept in so many crummy, unheated hotel rooms, shivered in so many way-stop depots and sat up in smoke-filled railroad cars so many nights that it was almost a relief when the show closed. On our way back to Fort Dodge, we stopped in Des Moines and found Lorin Guin there, out of work. He suggested that the three of us team up for independent vaudeville, doing one-act plays in conjunction with movies. Cecil was agreeable, so Lorin and I pitched in and made one-acters out of *Jack O'Diamonds* and several other standard rep bills and wrote several new plays of our own. One of these was a comedy-drama we called *Inspector Jimmy Donovan;* another, which had a good rube part in it for me (I called him Toby), was titled *The Bachelor's Baby*. Since movie houses often changed bills two or three times a week, we had to have fresh material for each show. Before the summer was over we had rewritten or written and were up in more than thirty one-act plays.

Inspector Jimmy Donovan, which had a lot of solid comedy, proved to be a highly successful opening bill, but in Lamoni, Iowa, we got only a few subdued chuckles during the show and hardly any applause at final curtain. I told Guin that we surely had flopped but when I went to settle up with the house manager he was very complimentary.

"That was a real fine play," he said.

"Well, the audience didn't seem to think so," I replied. "They sure didn't laugh very loud."

"They'd better not!" he declared. "I don't allow no loud laughing or cutting up in my theater."

All of the movie houses were very warm but in Marshalltown, where we played in a converted store on Main Street, the heat was practically unbearable. Guin and I discovered that a false floor had been built to provide an incline for the seats, so we drilled holes in it at intervals and under them installed electric fans and tubs of ice. It was a crude affair but the ice-cooled air forced up through the holes by the fans did help some and I often have wondered if that was not one of the first artificially-cooled theaters in America.

After Marshalltown, we played Hubbard, Iowa. The movie for the week did not arrive so we put on a whole evening's entertainment in place of it, doing three one-act plays—a comedy, a heavy drama and a farce. Business was so good that we decided not to play movie houses anymore but to go into opera houses, where we could get a higher percentage of the receipts. We booked three-night and week stands and did well until September, when Guin became ill. He went back to Des Moines, leaving Cecil and me high and dry again for the moment.

My brother Jap and his wife also were at liberty and so the four of us went out and played the same kind of one-act play shows for about a month. We did well, by my standards, but Jap was accustomed to making considerably more money, so late in October we closed the show and the four of us went back once more to Fort Dodge. Nothing else came up immediately but I got hold of some paper advertising a show, the name of which now skips me, and booked the opera house at Barnum, Iowa, for a one-night stand on Thanksgiving evening. That always was one of the big dates of the year and to secure the booking I told the manager I had a seven-people show. I really did intend to pick up three more people but there were none around as the date approached and I also could not find a seven-people show that in any way resembled the advertising, so I sat down and wrote a three-act play for four people. The four of us went out to Barnum with more than a little trepidation; we not only had promised seven people in order to justify a fifty-cent top but we also had an untried play. We played to a packed house and when the show was over the manager came down the aisle, beaming, and said: "That's the best play we've ever had in this house."

By this time my marriage with Cecil had soured for good. After the Barnum date she departed and I never heard from her again. Shortly after she left, Jap got jobs for himself, his wife and me on the Guy Hickman repertoire show and we joined just before Christmas. We played houses until about the middle of May and then moved under Hickman's tent—my first experience at that. We were rained out night after night and stayed at the first stand, Clarion, Iowa, three weeks in order to play one.

For some time I had been thinking that Hickman was not all he appeared. At first glance he was the picture of respectability —well dressed, well groomed, affable and a very persuasive talker —but, for one thing, there always seemed to be some perfectly logical reason why he could not pay my full salary every week. When time came to leave Clarion, Guy could not pay the hotel bill so he blithely left his elderly father as security, promising to send money from the next town. About three weeks later the old man showed up on the lot, but by then I was sure that it was not because the hotel bill had been satisfied. More likely, the manager got tired of being a patsy and threw him out. After that I pressed Hickman a little harder each week for a full paycheck but the shortage continued, so about the middle of July I quit.

On the way back to Fort Dodge I stopped off again in Des Moines and found that Lorin Guin's health had improved. We decided to go into Chicago and have a try at booking *Inspector Jimmy Donovan* in some of the vaudeville houses there. We hired a woman to do Cecil's part and although we were well received when we worked, bookings were so few that after three weeks or so I struck out on my own. I did a single act for a while in some of the minor vaudeville houses in Chicago, then got a job on another one-nighter, *Girl With a Million*. That lasted only four weeks, but I had been back in Chicago only a day or two when I landed the softest job I ever had, with Charles Mason in a vaudeville sketch called *Rudolph and Adolph*. The act was a boiled-down version of a mistaken identity farce involving two Germans who looked alike, in which Charlie had costarred in New York with Dan Mason, no relation. We played two-a-day vaudeville in week stands on the Orpheum Time throughout the winter of 1915-16 but, unfortunately, the United States was being drawn into World War I and anti-German sentiment was very high. Mason tried to convert his German characters into rubes in order to keep the act going but he simply could not get rid of his own thick German accent. Neither could he refrain from expressing, loudly, his pronounced pro-German sentiments. By May 1916 so many theaters were reluctant to book the act that Mason had to close and I went back to Chicago to look for work.

3

A day or so after I registered at the O. H. Johnstone theatrical agency Clyde Gordonier, who ran a tent repertoire show in downstate Illinois, came to town looking for a general business actor. After my experience with Guy Hickman, just about the last thing on earth I was looking for was another tent show but, never having been one to avoid the course of least resistance, I took the job.

Gordonier, a former barber, had married into the tent-show business. His wife and her mother and brother, the brother's wife and her sister and husband all were on the show. All were excellent musicians and above-average vaudeville entertainers. Grace Gordonier was a striking and accomplished leading lady and, in addition, had a dance act that would have stopped the show anywhere. At the climax of the act her long red hair streamed out behind her. Kate Pullman, a big-time vaudeville star of the period, paid Grace a thousand dollars for the act.

Topping off all this vaudeville talent, Clyde had a strong acting cast and an excellent repertoire of comedies. Two of the plays were conventional Toby vehicles and a third was *Out of the Fold*, which some writers have described as one of the first Toby plays but which really was not. The rube character in that play was called Evers Green and Clyde wisely did not change his name to Toby because he was not at all like Tobe Haxton in *Clouds and Sunshine*. He was just a rube—the kind that had been so popular with rural American audiences throughout the nineteenth century and at the beginning of the twentieth.

When I joined the show the comedian was a clever little fellow, not quite five feet tall, named Loren Sterling but he had to leave because of illness and Clyde gave his parts to me. While I tried to approach each characterization differently, I used the red wig and my Tobe Haxton makeup for all of them. Being in the Toby makeup, I discovered, provided an opportunity for more free-wheeling comedy than I had ever enjoyed before. Gordonier had a big old-fashioned circus tent with a steel center pole directly in front of the stage and to drive home a gag I often grabbed the pole and swung myself all the way around it. My between-acts specialties were mostly gagging acts but I also began working in parodies of popular songs. In one turn I told several stories and then, becoming serious, said, "Now ladies and gentlemen, I should like to sing for you my own version of that great old ballad, 'Let the Rest of the World Go By.'"

Leonora Connally, the pianist, started an arpeggio but I stopped her.

"I forgot to say this song I am singing tonight is accompanied by a three-piece orchestra," I said, "the piano, the player and the stool. Once again, professor."

Leonora began the introduction but once more I interrupted.

"And now, friends, I want to call your attention to the fact that our piano player plays on the white keys and plays on the black keys. I will sing in the cracks."

Leonora then went through the entire introduction and I sang something like this:

> To a dance I did go, where the gowns were
>   Cut low, held up only by a strap.
> One girl wore a dress, it was odd I confess;
>   It was made out of a map.
>
> Her chest was Brazil, her back Bunker Hill
>   And just a little below was Mexico.
> Her shoulder blades were Japanese;
>   On her bosom there was Greece;
> Her lips were Siam, her hips Hindustan.

I'm not quite certain 'bout her thighs,
For just then I saw my wife
And to save a lot of strife
I let the rest of the world go by.

I have always been glad I worked for Clyde Gordonier that summer. The big circus tent was one of the last of its kind, the blues reaching not only across the back of the tent but down the sides to the stage. Clyde still moved it from town to town on farmers' hayracks, as the old-time showmen had done. Yet he offered first-rate theatrical fare, setting a standard for other tent showmen to reach for.

The quality on stage largely was Grace Gordonier's doing. She knew her business and insisted on polished, fast-paced performances. Clyde did not know much about this end of the business but he was a wizard in front of the show. A small, sandy-haired fellow with an engaging grin, he made friends easily and had a sharp eye for promotional opportunities. About the time I joined him he learned that a billboard lithographer in Kansas City had been stuck with a large quantity of paper on a show called *Ishmael* that had failed. Clyde bought the entire stock—everything from half sheets to twenty-four-sheet stands—and then searched around until he found a New York bureau that had a script of the play. He asked me to produce it. This literally was impossible because the script called for a large cast and several elaborate settings and Gordonier had neither the people nor the capability of making so many scene changes, but he had all that paper on hand and he remained adamant.

"All right, Clyde," I said finally. "I'll write you an *Ishmael*."

Over a span of about a week I wrote an entirely new play, for eight people, following the original story line only in part. The advertising attracted big crowds and the play went over surprisingly well.

As Gordonier's tent season was ending, Charlie Mason reached me by telephone and asked me to rejoin him for a tour of B. F.

Keith houses around New York. Gordonier wanted me to stay with him for a winter house tour but the idea of getting to New York was more appealing. Charlie and I had played only a few dates, however, when he became desperately ill and returned to Michigan, where he died a short time later. I wired Clyde that I was available and he answered by return wire, telling me to join him in Oklahoma. We played to good business all winter but some of the people down there never quite took us to their bosoms. One Sunday, after a long overnight trip on a daycoach, we registered at a small town hotel and one of the actors, Jack Fleming, and his wife went straight up to bed. They hardly had fallen asleep when the hotel manager started pounding on their door.

"Get up! Get up!" he demanded. "You've got to get out of here!"

Jack stumbled to the door and asked what the racket was all about.

"You've got to get out of here," the man said. "The very idea! Coming in here and registering as man and wife!"

"Look, mister," said Fleming, angrily. "I've been married to this woman for twenty years."

"Don't tell me!" the hotel man said. "Don't tell me! Married folks don't go to bed in the daytime."

We checked into a hotel in Century, Oklahoma, the day after a musical tab company had left and when we all had signed the register the woman who ran the place said, with an air of resignation, "I wish you all would go ahead and double up now the way you're going to be. The last show people we had all took single rooms and half of them stayed empty."

One morning when we were rehearsing, a tall, spare stranger walked briskly onto the stage. He wore no overcoat, just a Palm Beach suit and a muffler.

"I should like to speak to the stage dir-ector," he said in a very

Shakespearean manner and in the deepest bass speaking voice I ever heard.

Since Gordonier wasn't there, I said I guessed I was the one he wanted to see.

"I am Clyde Tres-sell," he said, enunciating every syllable. "You no doubt have heard of me—Clyde B. and Minnie Tressell. We have traversed this territory repeatedly with our own company—tabloid of course. We have three chorus girls and one principal, myself, and if I do say so, it is the rottenest company that ever traversed the territory."

When it became apparent that what he wanted was a handout, not a job, we scraped together a few dollars and gave them to him. He departed with a courtly bow.

Years later, again in the dead of winter, I was sitting in the Johnstone agency office in Chicago when Tressell came in.

"I should like to re-gis-ter in this agency for an en-gagement," he announced to Helen Stanoline, who was in charge.

"What line?" Helen asked.

Clyde pulled himself up to his full height and in that deep, reverberating voice of his replied, "Light com-edy."

Old Clyde did finally land. There was a show called *Every Woman* and he snagged the part of Poverty in it. He was absolutely a star.

After a profitable winter tour following on the heels of a sparkling summer, Clyde Gordonier had every right to expect another good tent season in 1917. The cast remained practically unchanged. We had a repertoire of pretty good plays and we still had a lot of vaudeville. Yet we lost them. After a big opening night, attendance declined each successive night of every stand. Gordonier was bewildered. When the fellow who had been "holding script" left the show, Clyde asked me to take over direction and see what I could do. I was reluctant, but finally when he offered me a share in the profits and gave me complete authority behind the curtain line, including the right to hire and fire, I plunged into the job of tearing the show apart and putting it back together again.

To make money in repertoire, a company has to draw the same people, or a majority of them, back night after night. This requires not only enjoyable plays and satisfactory performances, but also the right sequence in the plays that are offered. Repertoire managers had many different ideas about this but I always have thought that Sam Spedden had the best one. He followed a very rigid formula:

> MONDAY (opening): A play with heart interest, a strong vein of comedy and "dress"—at least one act in which the entire company could appear in its finest attire. Most important, a play with "after draft"—the indefinable quality that made them say to one another, "Gee, that was good!" but not so much show that customers would get their fill and not want to come back.
>
> TUESDAY: A family comedy, to appeal especially to the women because it is the women who pull the men back the second time.
>
> WEDNESDAY: A hillbilly or mountain play—a change of pace, enjoyable but not too substantial.
>
> THURSDAY (feature night): A play with a strong, dramatic story line and settings to permit a more elaborate production than others in the rep; a play to be talked up from opening night.
>
> FRIDAY: A light comedy or warm-hearted story like *Jack O'Diamonds*.
>
> SATURDAY: A farce, to leave them laughing.

On the 1917 Gordonier show, our opener, *Her Fatal Wedding*, obviously had very little after draft and it was weak, also, on comedy. None of the other bills really met the need, either, but Clyde had an Alex Byers version of *Thorns and Orange*

Blossoms that had possibilities. The light comedy lead was a young fellow who had a huckleberry orchard. I changed the title to *Felix Finn, the Huckleberry King,* padded out the part with such priceless gags as, "We eat what we can and can what we can't," and made it the opener. I also rewrote *Human Hearts* extensively, beefing up the story line, adding some new dramatic scenes and toning down the comedy, and made it the Thursday night feature instead of the Wednesday show. Then I called daily rehearsals. In the face of considerable resentment from some of the old-timers, I required the cast to act in rehearsal the way they intended to act in performance, so that I could tackle interpretation of the characters as well as the spacing and the timing of the show. We worked over every bill in the repertoire and after each rehearsal our performance improved a bit. While this was going on, I cracked down hard on another aspect of the show that had got out of hand. Nearly everyone had become a gag artist. One fellow had a wonderful voice and stopped the show every time he sang "Mother Macree"; another did marvelous imitations of animal sounds, including a very exciting dog fight, but when they told jokes they put the customers under the seats. I told them the gags had to go, and when everybody began sticking to the thing he did best we regained the kind of polish that had won for Gordonier in 1916.

Within about three weeks the show began to click again. We opened to big crowds and built up, instead of losing, through the rest of the stand. This gave me a little free time and I got involved in another enterprise.

A fellow in Chicago named Sidney Anshell, who was selling peanuts and popcorn in the burlesque houses, discovered that by putting coins and other prizes in his packages he could attract extra business. He started the Universal Theater Concessions Company and put out a taffy candy called Frozen Sweets with "a prize in each and every package." A man named Grant set out to interest road shows in the product and his first stop was on the Gordonier show. Clyde was not at all impressed with Grant's pitch, but finally agreed to let him sell candy for fifteen minutes each night before opening curtain. Grant paid twenty-five dollars a week for the privilege and he and his wife stayed two or three weeks. None of us had any idea how much candy he was selling, or cared very much, but one day Grant told Ivan Stenberg, another actor, and me that he was making a substantial profit over the twenty-five-dollar concession. He wanted to get on to other shows so Ivan and I went to Clyde and arranged to take over the concession at the same rate. Since there was not time to dress and make up between the candy sale and curtain time we made up and dressed first, then sold our candy. (I think we were the first tent rep actors to do this, but it soon became the standard practice.) We made ninety dollars apiece the first week but, alas, did not have sense enough to keep our mouths shut. Clyde heard us bragging and took over the concession himself.

At the end of the regular season, Gordonier decided to take the show south for the winter. Our first jump was from Marysville, Missouri, to Ellsworth, Kansas, but through some mischance the baggage car containing the tent and other equipment did not arrive in time for the opening. Clyde made hurried arrangements to use a Chautauqua pavilion and we fortunately got through the week without rain. The tent, meanwhile, was shipped ahead to Waggoner, Oklahoma, and was already up when we arrived there on a bright and delightfully warm Sunday afternoon. I went up to my room to take a nap and when I came down again around five o'clock a first-class blizzard was raging. I went over to the tent and it was covered with nearly a foot of snow. We rigged up some stoves, banked dirt all around the tent to hold the heat in and played all week with snow on top of the tent. There wasn't a chance of moving it on Sunday and Clyde abandoned his southern tour. We played several Oklahoma towns and then went into Oklahoma City for an extended stock engagement at the Palace Theater. While there, we put up several Toby plays and one night after our performance the manager of the Palace, Raleigh Dent, came back to my dressing room to tell me how much he had enjoyed Toby.

"Neil," he said, "I think you ought to give serious thought to specializing in that kind of character."

4

Off and on ever since the United States began to get involved in the First World War, I had been trying unsuccessfully to get into the Army Air Corps, but in July 1918 Uncle Sam found me admirably suited for the infantry. I was drafted. They sent me to a replacement outfit at Camp Gordon, Georgia, and because the army was desperate for noncoms I had a meteoric military career. A few days after I got there my drill sergeant called me out of the ranks to put our platoon through close order drill. Having observed how the experienced noncoms performed, I naturally swung right into the act and was giving my buddies a real workout when a major rode up on a horse.

"Soldier, how much military service have you had?" he inquired.

"None, sir," I replied, "I just got here."

He looked me up and down and said, "I think you are a goddam liar," and rode off.

I advanced quickly from corporal to sergeant to top sergeant and along the way organized and staged a couple of shows for the troops. Shortly before the Armistice I was recommended for promotion to second lieutenant but that did not come through because all promotions were suspended when the war ended. I was discharged February 1, 1919, and on my way back to Fort Dodge to see my parents, I stopped over in Kansas City and landed a job with Fred Wilson, who by then was famous as a Toby comedian. This was my first experience with an entire repertoire of Toby bills and I was rather astounded that the audience did not tire of them before the end of the week. Wilson impressed me immensely. I could have finished the season with him but since I had not seen Mother and Dad in more than a year I left after ten weeks.

Clyde Gordonier was planning a series of house dates in Iowa before going into his tent for the summer and before leaving Wilson I wrote him that I would be at liberty. Clyde replied by return mail, offering fifty dollars a week, my old salary. I sent him a telegram asking for sixty and he replied by wire: DON'T MAKE ME LAUGH. MY LIP IS CRACKED. On the way back to Fort Dodge I stopped over in Boone, Iowa, to say hello to an old friend, George Flint, who managed the theater there. In the course of conversation I mentioned the exchange with Gordonier, not knowing that Clyde had booked Boone for one of his early dates on the tour. Flint immediately sent Gordonier a wire: UNLESS SCHAFFNER PLAYING COMEDY CANNOT PLAY SHOW. When I reached Fort Dodge a telegram was waiting: SIXTY OK. JOIN MONDAY. GORDONIER. I wired back: DON'T MAKE ME LAUGH. MY LIP IS CRACKED. SALARY NOW SIXTY-FIVE. That is what he paid me.

I came back from the army with a great many new ideas about how to improve the show and probably tried to move too fast. At any rate, I soon acquired a reputation as a swellhead. A bunch of us were sitting around a hotel lobby one afternoon and one of the women was working a crossword puzzle in a New York newspaper. "What's a four-letter word meaning ego?" she asked, then answered her own question, "Oh, I know. Neil." Anyway, Clyde and I began to have small differences about the show during the 1919 tent season and these became more frequent and heated during the house tour that winter. One thing led to another and early in the summer of 1920, not long after we had opened the tent season, we agreed to disagree. I went into Chicago and again registered at the Johnstone agency. In a day or two an order came through from a fellow named Izzy Weingarten, who owned a burlesque show on the American Wheel called *The Whirl of Mirth*. He wanted a light comedy juvenile straight who could sing and dance and though I was not much of a singer and the only dance steps I knew were the time-step and shuffle off to Buffalo, I took the job.

I joined *The Whirl of Mirth* at Waterloo and rehearsed while the show was doing a week of one-nighters through Iowa. Al Rackett, the orchestra leader, ran through my musical numbers with me, accompanying me on the violin at the tempo I was accustomed to in my tent rep specialties. My first performance was in a matinee at the Gayety Theater in Minneapolis and when time came for my first number Rackett hit the fastest tempo I had ever heard. The orchestra was down to the chorus before I got halfway through the verse. Gals in back of me were dancing like mad, so I skipped the song and started hoofing like I had never hoofed before.

"Why didn't you tell me you played things at breakneck speed like that?" I asked Rackett.

"Oh, I thought you knew," he said.

"Well, I didn't," I declared, "but you won't lose me tonight." And he didn't.

In many of the scenes in the burlesque show I worked with the principal comedian, Al Ferris, a slender little Jewish boy who did a German, or possibly Yiddish, dialect. He was known throughout burlesque as the cursing comic. If he did not get laughs where he expected them he came off stage cursing a blue streak.

"So you wanted to be an actor did you?" he would say to

himself in front of his dressing room mirror. "So you wanted to be an actor. You dumb S. O. B!"

When things went especially bad, Al would shout to everyone in general: "They'll never get me next season!" One night we were doing a scene in which I was supposed to hit him across the shoulders to emphasize a line. I accidentally hit him a little hard. "Why you S. O. B!" he snarled, loud enough to be heard in the audience. I went down to the footlights and said to Al Rackett, "They'll never get me next season!" Rackett started laughing and Ferris became so angry that he came down to the footlights, too, and shouted, "You don't believe me, huh? You don't believe me!" He got so agitated that there was no chance of going on with the scene so I took him by the nape of the neck and led him off the stage. Although it all was an inside joke, the audience roared.

Burlesque in those days was a very genteel form of entertainment and no off-color material was permitted. The manager fined Al two hundred dollars for that outburst at me, but it made no noticeable difference to him. Not long afterward, while we were playing Buffalo, he came storming off the stage, cursing himself, while I was completing a quick change from a soldier outfit to full evening dress for a song in a cabaret number. "They'll never get me next season!" he growled, and smashed his fist down so hard on the table that an opened can of face powder flew up into the air and came down on top of my head. It literally covered me, and at that instant the orchestra struck up the introduction to my number and I had to go on as I was.

To get around the Sunday blue laws of the period, vaudeville houses in the big eastern cities put on "sacred concerts"—regular vaudeville shows minus dancing acts—and when we got to Boston, Al Ferris and I discovered that talking acts were in great demand. One of the skits we did together in The Whirl of Mirth involved two soldiers, a tough noncom (me) and a stupid rookie.

Since the burlesque show did not operate on Sunday, Al and I hired an agent and he booked the soldier act into as many as five theaters on a Sunday, each at seventy-five dollars. To make it from one theater to another, Al and I hired a taxicab by the day and had the driver wait at the stage door to race us from one theater to the next. We continued playing Sunday vaudeville in Boston as long as *The Whirl of Mirth* was touring New England and when the show reached New York we again found all the Sunday work we could handle.

While *The Whirl of Mirth* was playing the Star Theater in Brooklyn, my actors' agent cousin, Ollie Logsden, came over to see the show. It was the first time we had met. She was a charming, witty young woman and obviously knew her business. I liked her immediately and apparently the feeling was mutual because the next time we had a visit she told me, in effect, she was going to do something to get me higher up in the show business scale. Soon thereafter she called me at the hotel one morning and told me to go at once to Keith's Fifth Avenue and see a man who had a vaudeville act called *The Rounder of Old Broadway*. I caught the first performance of the afternoon. It was a flash act—a miniature musical comedy—and the Rounder part, which was the star part, was right in my mitt. The owner of the act offered me the part, but there was a catch. He was to open the following Monday at the Palace and the only way I could make it was to jump the burlesque show without notice. I just could not do that and passed up my one and only chance to see my name in lights at the Palace.

A few weeks later we were playing Philadelphia and *Omar the Tent Maker*, a play starring Guy Bates Post, was there in its pre-Broadway shakedown. Leonard Lord, who had been on the Clyde Gordonier show one summer, was playing the second lead in it and I went over to see him. Leonard said Mr. Post wanted to make a change in one of the parts and needed a man who could step in immediately before the Broadway opening. As he described it, this was another sweet little comedy part that fitted me exactly but again I was faced with the proposition of jumping the burlesque show and I did not even talk to Mr. Post. Ollie Logsden tried to persuade me to give notice to *The Whirl of Mirth* and stick around New York. George M. Cohan was considering a revival of his play *The Tailor Made Man* and Ollie said she thought she could get me the lead, but I was about half sweet on one of the girls in the chorus and when the show started its swing toward the west I stayed on. While we were in Indianapolis I got a telegram from Ollie: GET IN HERE AT ONCE. HAVE TAILOR MADE MAN SET FOR YOU. For the third time in about as many months I turned my back on a chance to do a show on Broadway but that one, at least, probably was not a mistake. The Cohan revival lasted only about a week.

One of the little bonuses of working around New York and spending a lot of time in Ollie's office was that I got to meet the unforgettable Corse Payton. Every Iowa actor knew about Corse because he was one of the Centerville, Iowa Paytons. Centerville was the birthplace of perhaps more repertoire companies than any other town of its size in America. Out of it came the Hickman-Bessie Company, the Payton Stock Company, the Spooner Stock Company and the Al and Goldie Gorrell Stock Company. Corse was the Payton brother who went to New York. Other performers considered him possibly the world's worst actor but he had a knack of getting the public and some writers have called him "the king of repertoire." Corse always had at least one and sometimes several shows running in New York. He would lease a house and put up the short-cast play, *Bought and Paid For*, featuring himself in the comedy part of Jimmie Gillie. If business proved good he would hire other actors, put up another play and keep going. Then he would bring on another comedian and start a new show somewhere else. But

When I was prop boy at the Midland Theater, Fort Dodge, Iowa, 1904.

Caroline Hannah Schaffner, actress, at age six.

Mr. and Mrs. John Schaffner (Mother and Dad), 1925.

Brother Frank, known professionally as Jap LaCour, in *The Mark of Sicily,* one of his early repertoire parts.

Loren H. Guin, mentor, patient director, who opened a whole new world for me. As Josh Bumble in *Clouds and Sunshine,* where I first met Toby.

H.Murphy

11432 Aquq Vista St.

No.Hollywood Calif.

Mr.Neil Schaffner

Wapello

Iowa.

No.Hollywood Calif. May 15-64.

My dear Neil.

You are absolutely right.Your performance of "Toby
Haxton" in"Clouds and Sunshine" in Jan.1913 beat"Murphys'
Comedians" for at least three months.

The Toby epidemic on all my shows stems from a visit I made to
the No.2 co.where Fred Wilson was manager and comedian. The night
I arrived they were putting on a play called "Out Of The Fold".
It had such a hot Toby that,after the show,Wilson and I went into
a huddle and decided to exploit Toby to the fullest extent.

The reason I know you beat us to "Clouds And Sunshine" is because
of the fact that Alec Byres wrote me a letter about the play and
stated that you had made a decided hit in the part of "Toby".
The little old "come lately boys"must have their data slightly
muddled.

I note your letter to me was dated April 13. It reached me just
this morning. That makes it over a month late.

Am certainly glad to hear from you.

Please give my kindest regards to your lovely "Susie".

Sincerely

Horace Murphy

11432 Aqua Vista St.

Letter from Horace Murphy confirming the fact that I played Tobe Haxton
before he and Fred Wilson saw the commercial possibilities in making all
rubes "Toby."

Neil E. Schaffner — vaudevillian (in white shoes) in front of the Grand Theater, Minneapolis, 1921.

When I billed myself "The Polite Comedian," with Grace Connolly on the Clyde Gordonier show, 1917.

When I appeared as Yates in *Common Clay,* at the Princess Theater, Des Moines, 1925.

1926 — at least it was a tent.

Caroline as leading lady of the first Schaffner Players, 1926.

Publicity photo for the first Schaffner Players' tent repertoire company, 1926.

Susie Sharp (Caroline), Toby's costar, 1952.

A growing-older Toby, 1952.

I was Grandpa in *In Bed With Grandpa,* Schaffner Players' tent, 1955.

1953 — packing them in at Lewistown, Missouri, in spite of thickening television aerials.

1940 — prosperous enough at last to set up in lovely parks like this one in Monroe City, Missouri and . . .

. . . to move on our own fleet of trucks.

1962 — home of "America's Only Folk Theatre," on farewell tour.

A creaking Toby, with Susie, on farewell tour, 1962.

Our basic set, with changeable parts and panel inserts to meet almost any requirement, seen here in *The Return of Aunt Susan,* 1949.

One of eleven special sets designed by Jay Bee Flesner for *The Devil and a Woman,* 1957, and made possible by a special "wagon stage."

Wherever we went, they told *us* goodbye. Here, on my study wall in Sarasota, are some of the plaques, citations and mementos Caroline and I received on our last tour.

if business was bad he would put up a second short-cast play and close. He was a familiar figure along Broadway, wearing a red satin suit and ballyhooing his show as he strolled along.

When I met Corse in Ollie's office, he had just been married.

"I was drunk," he said, "and she took advantage of me when I was incapable of logical thought."

When *The Whirl of Mirth* closed in May 1921 Al Ferris and I played a number of dates with our soldier act in the Pantages houses, but Al was tired of traveling and being away from his wife. The National Theater, a stock burlesque house in Detroit, his hometown, offered him the principal comedian's spot and he took it, but before departing he introduced me to Bert Rose. Bert, who had been the featured comedian on the *Star and Garter* burlesque show on the Columbia Wheel, was interested in putting together a vaudeville act, but since midsummer was a poor time to launch a new act he suggested we postpone it until the fall. This was entirely agreeable with me because I figured I could pick up a few weeks in stock around Chicago. As usual, I dropped by the O. H. Johnstone office. They had just received an order from Otto Hitner, owner and operator of the show-boat Cotton Blossom. He wanted a man to play light comedy and do specialties for four weeks and offered forty-five dollars a week. I joined at Nauvoo, Illinois.

"Showboat" really was a misnomer for the Cotton Blossom, but for that matter so was it for all the floating theaters on the Mississippi at that time. The theater and quarters for the actors were built on a flat-topped barge, about thirty-five feet at the beam and perhaps eighty feet long, which was towed by a steam-propelled tugboat. The theater itself seated about three hundred and was rather nice, though the stage was terribly small. The foredeck of the barge served as the theater lobby. Tickets were sold from a window in one room of Hitner's quarters, forward on the port side, and as I remember the price was seventy-five cents for adults and a half-dollar for children over five. Not that this meant anything. Otto accepted almost any kind of produce in trade for tickets, which was a fine thing for the actors. We ate very well.

It was late afternoon when I arrived at the landing in Nauvoo and Hitner, a corpulent man with a ruddy face and a big voice, greeted me cordially. He wore a yachting cap and, like all other showboat impresarios, called himself "Captain."

"I want you to do your strongest dancing specialty after second act tonight," Hitner said.

"Dancing specialty?" I asked. "I'm not a hoofer. I do monologues and songs."

Hitner went to his apartment and returned with O. H. Johnstone's telegram. It said, SENDING NEIL SCHAFFNER, STRONG SINGING AND DANCING SPECIALTIES. Though plainly disappointed, he let me go on.

After two years on the road, my four weeks on the Cotton Blossom were idyllic. Actors had nothing at all to do except eat, sleep and perform in one show each night. We didn't even have to get out of bed, if we didn't want to, when the tugboat fired up shortly after daybreak and began huffing and puffing its way upstream to the next landing. Slowly as we moved, though, we usually reached our destination by noon and there was no sleeping for an hour after that because Hitner's steam calliope was fired up and the piano player gave an hour's concert. The blasted thing was so loud it could be heard for miles around; in fact, except for a single notice on the local post office bulletin board, the calliope was Hitner's only advertising.

When not fishing, I spent most of my time snoozing in a hammock on the foredeck of the tug. Only once did anything exciting occur. At Dallas City, Illinois, a sudden thunderstorm struck and the Cotton Blossom, tugboat and all, broke loose from the moorings and started drifting helplessly downstream. A half hour or more elapsed before the firemen could get up steam in the tug and we turned around and around in the current as a crowd gathered on the river bank. By the time we finally tied up again half the town was on hand. We had a fine house that night.

At the end of my fourth week, Hitner put up a short-cast play-for his downriver tour and I headed back into Chicago. Bert Rose and I started framing our vaudeville act. We met every day at a bench in Grant Park. Every time we got a comedy routine set, Bert would say the act still wasn't long enough so we'd put something else in. When we played our first date, at the Star Theater out on Milwaukee Avenue in Chicago, we had enough stuff for four vaudeville acts. We worked for forty-five minutes. The main part of the act had to do with a bottle of wine that Bert was supposed to have acquired by prescription from his doctor. I warned him that drinking Prohibition wine, even if legally secured, could be very dangerous because no one could be sure where it came from. However, since I had been a wine taster, I would be glad to give him my professional opinion. Between gags I tasted so much that the bottle soon was empty. Bert was a very funny man and the way he built up his frustration was hilarious. We made a big hit at the Star and the next day practically every ten-percent agent in Chicago came after us. We signed up with one of them and he booked us first into the Mc-Vickers, the Loew Circuit house in Chicago. This ordinarily was a cut-rate house, meaning that actors worked there at half-salary, but we went in at full pay.

The act opened with me walking on the stage, talking a blue streak, followed by Bert with the wine bottle tucked under his coat. As I got to the center of the stage I was supposed to turn and say angrily, "I don't want to talk to you at all." At our first performance at the McVickers, I stormed on the stage but when I whirled around the expression on Bert's face stopped me cold. He literally was white. "I forgot the bottle!" he whispered. Since that bottle was the whole act, he had to dash offstage and get it.

I tried to fill in but the audience could hear Bert running down those iron steps to the dressing room and back again and laughter broke out all over the house. When Bert came back on he was carrying the bottle straight in front of him, instead of under his jacket. We had a hard time getting back on track but the confusion seemed to catch the audience's fancy and we got a big hand when we were through. The next week, though, we played the Kedsie Theater on the west side and there died the death of a dog.

Meanwhile, our agent signed us to an intact vaudeville show containing five acts. From Chicago we went out to the West Coast and then worked all the way back to the East, playing the whole winter on the Loew Circuit. After that we played some of the B. F. Keith time, appearing on the same bills with many of the great vaudeville acts of the time, among them Fred Allen and Sylvia's Cockatoos. Allen was doing a mailman act. His partner came on stage and sang as Allen walked down through the theater in his mailman's uniform making the wry kind of comments that later won him fame on radio. Sylvia worked with a number of trained cockatoos, one of which carried on a regular gagging act with her. This one was simply uncanny. When its turn onstage was over it would sit on a perch backstage, never saying a word until closing night. Then as the actors began closing their trunks and as the scenery started down it cried out: "Goodbye. Hope to work with you again some time."

While Bert and I were on tour I got my fourth, and last, chance at Broadway. Earlier, while playing the Palace in Detroit with Al Ferris, I had become acquainted with J. C. Nugent, who was doing a tremendously funny monologue. He found out that I had dabbled in writing and one day brought a script to the theater and asked me to read it.

"I know I write good stuff, Neil," he said, "but they won't give me a chance in New York. One of these times I am going in there with my family and rent a theater and put on one of my shows. When I do I want you in my show."

"Oh sure, sure," I said, not really meaning it. I just put it down, as one would, as another actor dreaming about getting into New York.

To tell the truth, I was not terribly impressed with Nugent's play, but in the spring of 1922 I got a telegram from J. C.: HAVE LEASED BELMONT THEATER. GET IN IMMEDIATELY FOR REHEARSAL. Bert and I were booked for several weeks ahead and since I had visions of going into New York for three or four weeks of rehearsal for a show that would last only a night or two, I wired Nugent that it was impossible for me to join. The play? It was *Kempy*, starring J. C. himself and featuring his daughter Ruth and his son Elliott. It had a long run and the actor who got the part Nugent wanted me for was Grant Mitchell.

PART THREE

Fifteen Minutes

Fifteen Minutes

———————— ~~~ ————————

1

Bert Rose and I had never hit it off well personally and in the summer of 1922 we dissolved our act. I registered at the O. H. Johnstone office in Chicago and almost at once landed a job on the Fred Gordon tent repertoire show in Indiana. There I renewed an old friendship with Larry Johnson, whom I first had met on the Guy Hickman show. Larry made a living playing piano but his consuming ambition was to become a big-time playwright. He had written a number of plays, including *Putting It Over* and *Marriage of Elizabeth*, which were used by many repertoire companies, and while working for Fred Gordon he was rewriting a bunch of old plays for the George Winnett bureau in New York. Since he was blind in one eye and could see very little in the other, I typed his scripts for him and also helped some on the rewriting. When the Gordon show closed in September Larry proposed that we team up. He felt sure we could hit, and he may have been right. He later wrote several successful New York shows, including *It's a Wise Child*, which Belasco produced and which had a long run on Broadway, and spent several years writing movies that starred Marion Davies. With my acting know-how and his writing ability we might have made a good combination, but soon after we returned to Chicago an offer came through the Johnstone office for an engagement in Wichita, Kansas, with the North Bros. Stock Company and I took that.

Without realizing it, I crossed the divide in my career. From that point onward my course led not toward Broadway but toward Main Street—and toward Toby.

Working with the North brothers was an experience no actor could forget. Sport North, the star, was truly one of the great actors of the American stage and working with him in *The Great John Ganton* was one of the supreme privileges of my life; his portrayal of John Ganton was the most incisive and powerful that I ever witnessed. The entire season was one of pure delight for me, but my great center of interest became the ingenue, a beautiful little seventeen-year-old blonde named Ann Nielson. By Christmas I was thinking seriously about marriage.

One of the other actors in the North Company was George Lanshaw, a big good-looking fellow, who formerly had operated a tent show in Michigan. George had a heavy romance going with Louise Wellman, who had been his second business woman and piano player on the tent show, and it occurred to us that, with our intendeds, we had the nucleus of a good show. Ann could be our ingenue, I could do light comedy and George and Louise could play the leads. We had a handshake agreement to take out a tent show in the summer of 1923. There was one small hitch to our plan, but we soon remedied that. Neither George nor I had divorced our former wives, but we both filed suit at the same time; George testified for me and I testified for him and the judge granted both decrees. That cleared the decks for George to marry Louise, which he did later, but it brought trouble down around my head. Ann was Catholic. Her parents had opposed her marriage to a Protestant in the first place and unfortunately they arrived in Wichita for a visit just as news of my divorce got in the newspapers. They objected so violently that Ann broke our engagement.

At this great distance, it seems to me that the wounds healed quickly but this may have been due mainly to the fact that Billy Angelo entered the picture about then. Billy worked winters as a stagehand at the Princess Theater, where the Norths were appearing, but in summer he managed Angell's Comedians, a tent show owned by J. S. Angell. At one time Angell had been tent repertoire's biggest impresario, with eight shows on the road. He had a faculty for picking men with managerial ability, furnishing them with a tent outfit and starting them out as his partners. He made a lot of money and by 1923 had disposed of all of his shows except the Angelo unit and was living in retirement in California.

Angelo made me an attractive proposition to play leads and direct and when the basis for the Lanshaw & Schaffner partnership blew up I accepted. During the last weeks of the Norths' engagement I selected a repertoire of plays with strong light comedy leads and also wrote a new play for an opener, *Hard Boiled Hamilton*. The show did well but Billy Angelo's health was not good and early in August he had to leave. J. S. Angell came on from California to see what could be done about holding the show together and at once accepted my offer to take over for a half share in the profits. Angelo's wife, who was our leading lady, naturally left with him, and Jimmy Hahn, the hokum comedian, also chose that moment to take a job on another show. For a while it looked as if I had become a new manager without a show to manage. Fortunately, however, Mr. Angell had brought his son and daughter, Ted and Ruth, from California with him. Ruth was a very pretty girl and ambitious to become an actress so I made her the leading lady and turned Ted, a personable boy with a perpetual grin, into a Toby comedian.

Ruth and Ted took to acting with such enthusiasm that Mr. Angell proposed a fall house tour to give them some more experience. I booked a string of houses and brought on my brother Jap and his wife, Florence, and Florence's daughter by a previous marriage, Dorothy. While rehearsing I completed a new play, *The Vulture*.

My first impulse in writing this play was to capitalize on the great success then being enjoyed on Broadway by mysteries in which the audience as well as the actors were kept in ignorance about the criminal's identity until the very end. As I got into it, though, it seemed to offer a chance to develop some of the ideas about the Toby character that had been buzzing around in my brain ever since *Clouds and Sunshine*.

Nearly all of the authors who had appropriated Cal Herman's character had made Toby a clown or buffoon but I felt there was much more substance to him than that. To me, he was more like the boy next door. Like a lot of other lively young fellows, he might clown around some but this was youthful exuberance, not the expression of a simple mind. If at times he appeared to be brash and impertinent, this was not due to vanity but to an instinctive desire to puncture pretense or expose greed or hypocrisy. I saw him as pretty straightlaced morally—more of a Christian than those who wore their Christianity as a badge—and as having a native instinct for sorting right from wrong. And he was not just the unlettered farm hand or the town simpleton; he was anybody at all.

Toby Tolliver in *The Vulture* is a village boy who is trying to improve himself by studying fingerprinting by mail. He has a great deal to do with advancement of the plot and in the end, though appearing to have stumbled on the key rather than having deduced it, he solves the crime.

In a play like *The Vulture*, the action has to move fast. Actors must know their lines and come in promptly on cue. From the very start of rehearsals we had trouble with J. S. Angell, who was getting up in years and had a terrible time remembering his lines. He would go as far as he could and then say, "You know...," and sort of wave his hand in invitation to another actor to say something to keep the play moving. His part in *The Vulture* was Jenkins, the detective, and on our opening night, so help me, he forgot his name. On his very first entrance he stuck out his hand to Jap and stammered, "Name's uh ... uh ... uh, you know."

"Mister You Know," Jap responded, grabbing his hand, "I'm glad to know you."

Having got off to such a fine start, we maintained the record to the bitter end. In the last act Graham, played by Jap, is exposed as the Vulture and is killed by the French maid, Celeste, played by Dorothy. When Dorothy pulled the trigger the pistol did not fire but Jap, being the experienced hand he was, clutched his chest and cried, "Maxim silencer! Silent as the night and deadly as a rattlesnake!" He fell across the couch. Dorothy was a little too slow on the uptake. She kept pulling the trigger and just as Jap was expiring the gun went off.

As time went on we managed to avoid anything as bad as that and J. S. finally learned his lines, but we did very little business. Night after night I approached curtain time with my stomach in knots because we never knew until then how much audience we would have. Early in November we played a fine little upstairs opera house in Clearfield, Iowa, and on the first night as usual we opened the front door about seven o'clock. Show time was eight fifteen. Just before calling Half Hour I peeped out around the curtain to see how the house was coming and exactly two people were present. At the Fifteen Minutes call there were no more than half a dozen and, unable to stand it any longer, I went out front to the box office where the house manager, a high-school teacher, sat reading a newspaper.

"Doesn't look like we're going to have much of a crowd," I said.

The manager looked surprised. "What's the matter?" he asked. "Are you ready to start?"

"Yes, we're ready to start, but we don't have any audience."

"Of course you don't have any audience," he said. "I haven't rung the bell yet."

With that he walked out on a little balcony at the front of the theater and struck a big gong. People came pouring out of stores all around town and in a few minutes we had a packed house. We opened with *The Vulture* and after the show I went out front to settle up and asked the manager how he liked it.

"Oh it was good, it was good," he said, "but I like a play with a well-defined plot."

Each night as the week progressed he said the same thing. On closing night we did *The Panther*, a hash-up by one of Alex Byer's hack writers in Chicago. Originally it had been a large-cast play and I had slashed characters out of it until it was disjointed to say the least. Sure enough, after the show that night the manager said, "Now, *there's* a well-defined plot."

Around New Year's 1924 we reached the Drake Avenue Theater in Centerville, Iowa, and there I met the Payton brother who stayed home. His real name was Elbert but everybody called him Slivers. Many years earlier he had operated a medicine show and people around Centerville said he still was making a tidy living selling his nostrum by mail to his former show customers, but the pride of his life was the Drake Avenue Theater. A big line formed in front on our opening night and I dropped by the box office, where Slivers himself was selling tickets. He was barking at everybody.

"So! You old tightwad!" he would say. "Finally broke down and decided to take the woman to a show, huh? Suppose you want the cheapest seats in the house, huh? Go ahead! Speak up! What is it you want?"

This was just an act, of course, and everybody in Centerville loved it because they loved Slivers. They loved us, too, but unfortunately they were the last. After Centerville business was so bad that we abandoned week-stand repertoire and went into circle stock. This is a form of entertainment that was popular in many small midwestern towns. The idea was for a company to base in one town and then work in a "circle" around it— playing six different towns on the week, returning to each town on the same night week after week. On our opening week the Wednesday night town was Oquawka, Illinois, and we had about two hundred people in the house, which was not bad considering what we had been doing in rep, but when we came back the following week we did not sell a single ticket. A new dance hall was opened that night and just about everybody in town went there. We skipped Oquawka after that but the town that replaced it was not much better. After several unsuccessful weeks on the circle we went back to week-stand rep and just stumbled through the rest of the spring. Getting back under the tent was a relief.

In organizing the company for the 1924 tent tour I was lucky enough to pick up several acting people who doubled in brass. We started the season with a very good orchestra and I began searching for ways to capitalize on it. This was hard to do because all tent shows until then put their orchestras down on the ground in front of the stage, where no one could see them. I built a platform at one side of the stage and featured the orchestra in a half-hour concert before the opening curtain every night. (In a few years the orchestra platform became standard with all tent shows but I think we were the first.) The reaction was so good that I started costuming the musicians in harmony with the numbers they played. One night they wore Chinese costumes and played only numbers with Chinese themes; another night they played western tunes and dressed as cowboys. These things cost money, of course, and J. S. dragged his feet all the way but our business improved steadily and I guess J. S. was satisfied. When we closed the tent he went back to California for the winter. I blew most of my share of the season's profits on a new Franklin car and went to Fort Dodge for a visit. While there I took in all the shows in town.

2

A tabloid musical comedy company called Al Russell and His Sizzling Cuties was appearing at the Lyric Theater and at the end of the chorus line there was a little redheaded cutie who caught my eye. When the performance ended I made a beeline backstage and managed to meet her.

Caroline Helen Hannah was her name. She was born in Orange, Texas, and grew up in DeRidder, Louisiana. She attended Louisiana State University and taught school for a year, then studied expression at the Horner Institute of Fine Arts in Kansas City, being the first graduate of its School of Expression. Before going into musical tab as a dancer, she had been a "dramatic reader" in Lyceum and Chautauqua. These things I learned on daily visits backstage. On Sunday I went to church with Mother and, much to my surprise, there was Caroline. I introduced her and she made such an immediate hit that Mother invited her out for dinner. Caroline and I spent the whole afternoon discussing show business and I laid it on pretty thick about the tent show I was managing during the summer. Caroline confessed that she very much wanted to get out of the chorus line and become a dramatic actress and I talked at some length about repertoire being the place to get sound training. I practically assured her a job on Angell's Comedians. We saw one another only once or twice after that, though, because Clyde Gordonier offered me a job in a stock company he had put into the Princess Theater in Des Moines. This engagement lasted until the middle of December and after the holidays I joined the Nat and Verda Cross Company for a ten-week house tour in Oklahoma.

Through most of the winter I worked on a couple of plays. One was an expansion of the little four-people show I had done for Jap, Florence, Cecil and me back in 1914; I called it *What Every Daughter Learns*. The other was a play centered around a cantankerous old Mr. Big who has been so mean to all his relatives and friends that the whole town hates him. Finally he becomes ill and his relatives convince him he is going to die. He starts giving money to the church and to his relatives and to the poor and generally trying to be as righteous in his final hours as he has been wicked through the rest of his life. I called the play *The Old Grouch*. In it Toby Tolliver is the doctor's office boy.

Caroline and I corresponded all through the winter and on March 6, 1925, I wrote her in Sioux City, where she was appearing at the World Theater, and made a firm offer.

> I have to hire two people and I immediately thought of you as the ingenue. Here is your chance to get a start in the dramatic game. I don't believe we ever discussed salary, but I will offer you thirty dollars to start and if you make as good as I think you will I'll raise it to thirty-five.
>
> You will play a pretty nice line of parts and I will want you to get up in some double specialties with me. You will play Dorrie in "What Every Daughter Learns," and a swell wisecracking part in "The Old Grouch," a flapper in "Taming of a Flapper" and I don't know just what else. I will give you all the coaching I can and do all in my power to make you a success.
>
> I suppose the thought has come to you, sometimes, that I was talking merely to hear myself spout when I was in Fort Dodge, but I meant everything I said, and have been thinking of you all the time.

Caroline accepted by return mail and, naturally, asked for an advance. She joined at Murray, Iowa, on April 27. During rehearsals and at the start of our tour we had dinner together every night and often went for a late evening ride in the Franklin. I enjoyed it all so much that it made me uneasy. One night I stopped the Franklin on a country lane and told her there was a matter of business that I had to discuss with her.

"You know, of course, that I've played this territory for a number of years," I said. "For business reasons, it will be necessary for me to renew friendships with people in the towns we play and, on occasion, I will have to take out another young lady. You and I will still be together part of the time, of course, but you must understand that this is the arrangement that we will have for the rest of the summer."

Caroline sat very still for several minutes, then in a voice that was not altogether calm she said she had thought over what I had to say and was prepared to respond.

"Well, go ahead and respond," I said.

"I completely understand the business part of what you say," she said, "and of course you are perfectly free to go out with any of your lady friends any time you want to. However, you should understand that you cannot go out with them and with me also. If I am not going to be all of it, I'm not going to be in it at all. You can just make up your mind which you prefer."

Under those circumstances, business never seemed to require me to date other girls. In July, Mother and Dad came to visit the show in Jefferson, Iowa, and one afternoon Mother asked, "Neil, why don't you marry that girl?" That very night I proposed and about a week later, on July 24, 1925, we drove over to Sac City and got married. It was not the most solemn of weddings. We were doing a play that had a wedding scene, in which the ceremony is performed by an old squire who concludes with the line, "I now pronounce you man and wife. Two dollars please." Caroline and I were married by a justice of the peace who must have seen the play. He went through the ceremony in a most perfunctory manner and when he got to the end of it, without so much as taking a breath, he said, "I now pronounce you man and wife two dollars please." That broke me up.

When Caroline joined for rehearsal in March, we had an understanding that a part of her salary would be withheld each week until the advance had been repaid. We were married on a Friday. On the previous Saturday I had withheld the last installment on her advance, so the day after we were married she would have been entitled to her first full paycheck. She has maintained ever since that I married her just to avoid paying her for that week's work.

During my two previous summers with Angell's Comedians, one night on practically every week had been wrecked by a free concert by the town band, but at the beginning of the 1925 season I conceived of a way to eliminate this competition. In each town I offered to do a benefit for the band association, and since the bands were supported by popular subscriptions among the merchants, my proposition fell on receptive ears. I gave the associations ten percent of our gross; in return they furnished us lot, license and lights and, instead of presenting the weekly concert, the band played a few numbers each evening in front of our tent. Our business doubled. In towns where we had done six or seven hundred on the week in 1924 we jumped to twelve or thirteen hundred. On July 4 in Baird, a town Angell had never played before, we took in five hundred and forty dollars— the biggest single day's business in Angell's history. It was too good to last.

Early in the summer the Actors Equity Association opened a concerted drive to organize tent repertoire. I was strong for Equity—in fact I was its member No. 720—and naturally wanted to make Angell's Comedians an all-Equity Show, but J. S. Angell opposed the idea. No amount of cajoling would make him change his mind. About the first of August Clarence Sterling, the traveling representative of Equity, came on the show in Britt,

Iowa, and told me that I either had to make the show all-Equity or leave it. Having just walked into half-interest in a show making so much money, I naturally hated to give it up, but J. S. was adamant and there was nothing I could do but quit. Fortunately, it was a friendly parting. J. S. understood my position and I understood his.

Caroline and I went into Des Moines for a few days of belated honeymoon and while there heard about a tent show, known as the Baldy Wetzell Company, that was in trouble. Baldy Wetzell had been a rather famous piano player in western Iowa but his tent show had not done well and he apparently had just walked out, leaving the outfit with the actors. They were trying to keep going but none among them knew anything at all about managing a show. Caroline and I drove out to Colfax, Iowa, to look it over. The players were mostly inexperienced but they had a lot of good music and as a group were pretty clever. With good management and direction, I thought they had the potential for a good show. I made them a proposition to take over and they jumped at it. We booked several towns west and south of Fort Dodge and did well until the end of September. Our last date of the season was at the fair in Fonda, Iowa, and on our closing night, a tremendous storm came up and blew the tent to ribbons. That ended the Baldy Wetzell show, but I had an idea that there would be an opening in Fort Dodge for a show doing abbreviated, or tabloid, scripts to run an hour in conjunction with the movies. I sold the idea to J. B. Julius, the manager of the Strand Theater, and he signed us for ten weeks at five hundred dollars a week. All of the tent show cast stayed on and I hired four additional people.

We called the show The Neil E. Schaffner Players and opened with a matinee performance of *The Vulture*. The most important prop in the play was a long black robe worn by Graham in the first two acts and as Caroline and I were walking toward the stage entrance at the Strand I suddenly realized that we did not have the robe. "Vulture robe!" I exclaimed, pointing my finger at her. We tore back out to the house, picked up the robe and barely got back in time for the opening curtain. From that time on when either of us forgot anything of importance we looked at the other, pointed a finger and exclaimed, "Vulture robe!"

The Neil E. Schaffner Players were an immediate success at the Strand, standing them out at every performance. Mr. Julius held us over two extra weeks and would have kept us longer, but before signing us he had contracted for a big feature picture on a percentage basis and he could not afford both it and us. We went out to play repertoire in Centerville, Ottumwa and other towns in southern Iowa, most of which at the time had reputations as being terrible for rep shows, but we did excellent business. Caroline and I also lived too well. When we got to Ottumwa I discovered we had exactly nine dollars and fourteen people to pay by Saturday night. Luckily, we packed them in there and by the time we had played Oskaloosa, Grinnell and several other towns we were fairly solvent again. But then the weather became terrible. Temperature dropped below zero and snow piled up until you could hardly get to town on muleback. Our business went from bad to horrible and to add to other complications Caroline discovered she was pregnant.

Frank North joined us to do advance work and I asked him to look around for a theater in one of the larger cities. I felt sure that if we could find the right place we could go in with a popular price and do well and Frank came up with a suggestion that sounded ideal. In Kansas City the Auditorium, a beautiful old opera house, had been standing vacant for years but the owner was willing for us to go in there. We were so confident that we would spend the rest of the winter there that Caroline and I rented an apartment, but we opened on a Sunday night to a gross of only fifty dollars. Attendance went down from there. In the middle of the week I wired old Slivers Payton up in Centerville and asked him to loan me a hundred and fifty dollars and let me jump the show to the Drake Avenue Theater. He wired me the money and told me to come on. There was not time to do any billing but Slivers did get an ad in the evening paper and when we got into Centerville, late in the afternoon, I drove around the city, announcing through a megaphone: "Schaffner Players at the Drake Avenue Theater Tonight." We opened to an almost full house and had good business through the rest of the week.

"After this," Slivers told me, "stay in your own backyard."

While playing Centerville I got in touch with Mr. Julius in Fort Dodge and he agreed to book us into the Strand again for three weeks, but after the Kansas City fiasco I was not able to pay salaries. I called the company together and told them what the situation was. All of them said they would stay with us but after the meeting they all came to me, one by one, and told me they were leaving. Being left high and dry with no show, Caroline and I went back to Fort Dodge, which of course always was a refuge, and Caroline swore she never again would leave Iowa, winter or summer.

3

The question before the Schaffners in the spring of 1926 was not whether to take out a tent show but how.

Somewhere I heard that Clyde Gordonier, who then was operating several stock companies up in Canada, had the insides of his old tent outfit stored over at Earlville, Illinois, so I proposed in a letter that he find a tent and rent the whole outfit to me for fifteen percent of my gross. He took me up. The tent he provided was a very old, dirty, gray circus tent that had been cut down and made into a dramatic end. When it was stretched it looked thin enough for me to poke a finger right through it, but it was a tent and that is the first ingredient of a tent show. Thus equipped, I wrote my brother Rome, who was doing well in business in St. Paul, and asked if he would loan me five hundred dollars to get started. He sent a check by return mail.

Because the mortality rate was high among the tents and because The Schaffner Players was a new show, people who had worked on the better repertoire shows were rather hesitant to take a chance on us, but we finally put together a fair company. Among them were Frank Colton, who had grown up on the Jessie Colton show and knew all about tents, and Chester Espey and his wife. We also hired a father, mother, daughter and son—the Dodd Family—for our orchestra. I ordered some special one-sheets on *The Old Grouch*, *The Vulture* and *What Every Daughter Learns* and advertised the show widely around Earlville, where we rehearsed. By opening night most of the money Rome had loaned me was gone and by midweek it was clear that we would not do enough business to move the show and lift the actors out at the end of the week. In desperation I wired Rome for another hundred and fifty dollars and he sent it by Western Union money order.

On our second stand, Mendota, we did very little better. Dozens of carloads of people sat outside listening to the orchestra on opening night but when the concert ended most of them drove off. But the next day we got a sort of reverse English break. A representative of the Union Concession Company of Chicago, Clarence Balleras, came on the show with something new—an "outside bally" approach to the candy sale. The Frozen Sweets candy we had sold on the Gordonier and Angell shows had prizes in every box, some good and some not so good, but with the purchase of a certain amount of candy, Union Concession provided an assortment of more desirable prizes—French dolls, kitchenware and the like—which could be displayed on the stage as an inducement to buy. In every tenth box there was a coupon that identified a prize on the stage. Balleras said that even with a small crowd like we had on opening night we ought to clear at least thirty dollars a night on the candy. To my amazement, he also said that if I needed a little money he thought his company would make me a loan, so I bought a stock of candy and went to work. That night after the orchestra concert we opened the curtains to show the prizes and then I came out in my Toby makeup for the pitch.

"Now folks, we're gonna have our candy," I said, speaking from the orchestra platform. "If you'll look over there on the stage you'll see a lot of swell premiums. See all them prizes? There's French dolls and electric lamps and blankets and hundreds of other swell prizes. Now all them things we carry from town to town. The only reason we got 'em on display is to make you think you're gonna win one of 'em—after all, this is a money-making scheme! But I want to make one thing clear: tonight, at this performance only, every cent taken in at this candy sale goes for the benefit of the poor—poor Mrs. Schaffner. I ain't gonna tell you there is a prize in each and every box 'cause there ain't. If there was I'd go broke, but every once in a while there is a box with a coupon in it. If you git one of them coupons, just bring it down to the stage and the lovely lady will give you whatever it calls for. Now the price of the candy is the same old price—just fifteen cents a box—but tonight as a special inducement, I'm going to let you buy two boxes for thirty cents."

Balleras was right. The candy profit amounted to around thirty dollars a night in Mendota and built up somewhat as our crowds improved at the next two stands but we still were not meeting expenses. I took a big chance and wired the Union Concession Company, asking for a loan of two hundred and fifty dollars, and they came through the same day. That money kept us going through two or three more indifferent weeks in Illinois and made it possible for me to buy newspaper ads in Mt. Pleasant, Iowa, in advance of our week there. I had played Mt. Pleasant with both the Gordonier and Angell shows and the people apparently remembered me favorably because we had a real good week. For the first time we took in more than we paid out.

Our Wednesday night show was *The Old Grouch*, which I talked up big on Monday and Tuesday nights, and when we opened the doors at seven o'clock we had a long line out front. Banks of clouds were building up all around but the people did not seem to mind and we gladly admitted them to the tent. Just before time to start the show the storm hit. Caroline, who had stopped working on stage because of her impending motherhood, was selling tickets out front and I was taking up tickets on the reserved seat section. When the first thunder crashed I went out to see about her; she was nowhere in sight. I raced around to the back of the lot and there she was, huddled down in the back of our car with our jackbox in her arms, trying to keep out of sight. We had taken in about two hundred dollars and her first instinct was to hide and not let anyone take it away from her, show or not. Fortunately, the storm passed in a few minutes and we went on with the performance—not only saving that night's receipts but probably saving The Schaffner Players as well. (We still have that jackbox. It is just a plain little leather satchel but every cent we ever took in with our own show was first put in it.)

My big inspiration at Mt. Pleasant was a Charleston contest. In the small Negro community there I found several youngsters who said they knew how to do the dance, which was all the rage then, and for three nights I talked up an all-Negro competition on Friday night. We packed the house. The kids were so good that when we played Mediapolis the following week I sent my car back to Mt. Pleasant for them and they packed the house for us again. The Mediapolis week was so good that we paid back salaries and brought all of our accounts up to date. The promise was very bright when I took Caroline and her mother, who had been traveling with us, over to Columbus Junction the following

week and put them on a train to Kansas City. Caroline wanted
to await the birth of our child there.

While playing Mt. Pleasant I finished another Toby play,
Where Is My Teddy, which in a mild way tried to say that dis-
crimination because of race is wrong. The hero is a gypsy boy
who falls in love with the local schoolteacher and, of course,
encounters hostility because of his unfamiliar racial and cultural
background. Toby plays a big, if bumbling, part in bringing
about the happy ending.

In time *Where Is My Teddy* became one of the three plays
given the largest number of performances in tent repertoire—the
other two being *Sputters* by George Crawley and *The Awaken-
ing of John Slater* by Charles Harrison. I have heard it said that,
because of the large number of tent shows on the road in the
twenties and early thirties, these three plays each were performed professionally more even than that ancient perennial,
Uncle Tom's Cabin. I cannot truthfully record, however, that
Where Is My Teddy made immediate history for The Schaffner
Players of 1926. We introduced the play into the rep as we
moved up through the rich center of Iowa—the "real Iowa,"
someone has said, of fertile fields of corn and wheat, of white
houses and big red barns and tall silos—but our attendance went
steadily downhill until we reached New Sharon, which was the
hometown of the Espeys. There we had an enormous week and
there, also, I got a telegram informing me that I was the father
of a boy. We named him Rome Lee—Rome for my brother who
had financed our show, and Lee for Caroline's late father. I was
so elated that I traded for a big beautiful new Nash car, in the
process trading payments of forty-three dollars a month for payments of sixty.

Caroline came back on the show and took up her parts again
when Rome Lee was thirteen days old and by that time we again
were not taking in enough money to pay bills. At Caroline's in-

sistence, we gave four notices but on the same day I received a letter from George Lanshaw. He had closed his show up in Michigan, where the season was shorter than in Iowa, and wanted to know if we could use him and his wife. I wired him to come on, thus replacing four people with two. The Lanshaws were excellent additions to the cast but the improved quality of the show seemed to have little, if any, bearing on the number of customers we could attract. For our closing week we booked Clio, a little town at the southern edge of Iowa, and it rained every day. Business was pitiful. When we had paid all the actors, Caroline and I had less than five dollars left.

On the morning after closing, Caroline and I were sitting in a restaurant trying to figure out what to do next when Frank Colton walked in and sat down at our table. After some awkward conversation he asked me whether I had any money.

"No, Frank," I said, "I haven't."

He pulled a twenty-dollar bill out of his wallet, handed it to me and walked out without a word. With that I was able to get my family back to Kansas City.

Once more I wrote to Mr. Julius in Fort Dodge and again he booked us into the Strand Theater to do tabloid versions of our plays between the movies. On the strength of that booking we put together a company with ourselves, the Lanshaws and one or two others but the show did not compare with our earlier one and we lasted only four weeks. Meanwhile, I wrote all over for another booking and finally, during our last week at the Strand, got an offer from the World Theater in Sioux City. I was so anxious to land it that I signed a real sucker contract; it provided that the first thousand dollars on the week went to the house and everything after that was split equally. To acquire money to move the actors we sold the new Nash for two hundred dollars and an old 1919 Dodge touring car. We attracted fair crowds in Sioux City but the house share ate up most of the receipts and we barely were able to hang on for ten weeks. Then, for want of other bookings, we had to disband the company.

Caroline and I went back to Kansas City and when we got there we found a letter from Ed Dillon, who had been a leading man on the Gordonier show. He said he had a guaranteed stock engagement for ten weeks in Tuscaloosa, Alabama, and offered ninety-five dollars a week for the two of us. We immediately shipped four trunks to Tuscaloosa and leaving Rome Lee with Caroline's mother, took off for Alabama in the Dodge. We arrived a few days after New Year's 1927 and found that Dillon's arrangement was with a brand-new sixteen-hundred-seat theater called the Casino. Everything looked rosy. During rehearsal, however, we learned that Ed did not have a ten-week guarantee, as he had stated, but a two-week guarantee with options for eight more. There is a whale of a difference between the two.

We opened to fewer than a hundred people and during the guaranteed two weeks we never played to more than two hundred. After that, salaries stopped. Dillon booked a circle for stock and in two towns out of the six we did very good business. On the first trip around the circle we played *The Vulture* to a packed house in Greensboro. For the second week Mrs. Dillon insisted on *Faith and Mary Ann*, a droopy, weeping-willow sort of play in which she had a long, drawn-out crying lead. The Greensboro theater manager spent a lot of money advertising "Toby in the great comedy, Faith and Mary Ann" and he was enormously displeased when he discovered Toby was not in that play. At the end of the first act he came storming backstage.

"You put on that red wig and get out there," he told me, shaking his finger under my nose. "These people are getting hostile. They came here to see Toby—and that's what they're going to see!"

I quickly put on Toby makeup and went out and did a specialty, working for half an hour or longer. I told every joke I knew and got a wild reception. Mrs. Dillon was not very fond of me after that but when we returned to Greensboro we had a Toby bill.

In Demopolis we played in a motion picture theater three weeks in a row but people were not going to the movies on other nights so the manager canceled us. We played another town the next week and the manager came over and begged us to come back. "People are so sore at me now they won't come to my theater at all," he said.

Greensboro and Demopolis held up every week but, alas, two towns do not make a successful circle. Dillon decided to try week-stand repertoire but in the first stand, Talledega, he took in only enough to pay our hotel bills. He could not even afford to ship our trunks to the next stand, Childersburg, so we took along only the clothing we would need for the first bill or two. Caroline and I transported as many of the company as could pack into the Dodge. There being no money between us, we checked into a second-rate American plan hotel, hoping to get a good Sunday dinner—only to learn they did not serve meals on Sunday. Ed Dillon swung into action.

"How terribly disappointed we are," he told the woman who ran the place. "We have been hearing about your wonderful meals ever since we came to Alabama and we drove over here this morning especially to have Sunday dinner with you."

"Oh is that so?" the landlady asked, obviously impressed. "Well, I guess we can scare up a dinner of sorts."

That's just what it was. There were some nondescript pieces of leftover chicken, some tasteless vegetables and coffee that was indescribably bad. As we were forcing down the last of the coffee the landlady said she felt sorry for us, traveling around as we did, because it was so hard to get anything good to eat.

"Now my husband and I took a trip last summer and you know we couldn't get a decent cup of coffee anywhere," she said. "I could hardly wait to get home and get my old coffee pot out and make a decent cup of coffee."

Dillon had booked Childersburg under the auspices of the P. T. A. and we went in there full of hopes for a big advance sale. It turned out to be only about a dozen tickets, and nobody else walked in off the street. After that night, Caroline and I decided that if we were going to starve we might as well do it in familiar surroundings and although Ed became very angry with us we left the show. At that moment we did not have the slightest idea how we might get out of town but the next morning I went over to the post office and there was a letter from Larry Johnson. When we had parted back in 1922 Larry had offered to try selling some of my plays for me, splitting the proceeds. He had sold *The Vulture* to the Dennison Play Company, along with some of his, and my share came to two hundred and fifty dollars.

Caroline and I slipped back into Talledega and pushed and pulled our wardrobe trunks out into the alley behind the theater. Somehow we wedged two of them into the back seat of the Dodge and tied one to each running board. Then we slipped out of Alabama like a couple of gypsies who had just stolen the farmer's best horse.

Back in Kansas City, I worked night and day typing scripts of *The Vulture, The Old Grouch* and *What Every Daughter Learns* and managed to lease them for the 1927 season to several repertoire shows. We took in about two hundred dollars over and above our groceries. Meanwhile I corresponded with George Lanshaw and we agreed to pool our slender resources and tour the old Angell's Comedians territory in Iowa as the Schaffner-Lanshaw Players.

4

At the end of the 1926 season we had stored the old Gordonier tent, sopping wet, in a barn at Clio. Sure that it would be ruined, I wrote everyone I knew trying to find a satisfactory used tent but had no luck. George Lanshaw and I went to Clio a week before we were to start rehearsals and dragged the old tent out of the barn. It had surprisingly little mildew and rot. We sewed up the rips and stretched it out carefully and it did not look too bad, but to make it look more like a repertoire tent we built a marquee out of some white Indianhead muslin. We had everything ready to go by Friday before our Monday opening. Late that afternoon a heavy storm came up and George and Louise, Caroline and I watched from the hotel as the storm uprooted trees and did a lot of other damage, expecting to see the tent go at any minute, but the good Lord was with us. It did not even spring a seam.

We had a poor opening at Clio, and for an odd reason. During our closing week in 1926 a star player on the Clio High School football team, a boy nicknamed Bulldog, had helped us with the tent. He said he wanted to travel with the show and I told him that if he still felt that way when we came back in 1927 I would take him along. People told us that Bulldog talked of nothing else all winter long, but a week before we returned to Clio he was killed in an automobile accident. That put a damper on the whole town.

"Every time I come near that tent I think of Bulldog," one man told me, "and I just lose my appetite for a show."

Still worried that the old Gordonier tent would not last out the season, I kept writing letters as we moved from Clio toward our regular territory and at last Sam Spedden, who long since had retired, wrote that he would sell me a tent he had used on a medicine show which he ran after leaving repertoire. It arrived while we were playing New Sharon. Unfortunately, it was not nearly big enough; our chairs filled the entire area, making it necessary for us to set the blues out under the stars. (We moved the sidewall out ten feet to encircle them.) The tent was beautiful from the outside but when we got it up sunlight revealed nine million holes caused by dry rot. We nevertheless featured our "big waterproof tent theater" in our advertising.

"Big waterproof tent, huh?" said a town boy one day after he had helped us put it up.

"Well, son, that shows you how much you know about tents," I said. "It is treated in such a way that if it rains the water runs around the holes."

Newspapers and humor magazines of that period were full of cartoons and jokes about flappers, rumble seats, petting and the like and along the way I finished a new play, *Why Girls Walk Home*, that capitalized on that. In it Toby is a hog buyer who drops into a roadhouse along the highway and gets mixed up with a bunch of gangsters. We introduced it during Fourth of July week and it was a big hit. We advertised as heavily as we could and business built up steadily all through the summer. Toward the end of the season we had two fantastic weeks.

At Floris, Iowa, there was an annual fox hunt—Iowa style, that is, not the fancy dress things they have in England and back East. They hunted the foxes at night. We made a deal to set up our tent at the headquarters of the hunt, about three miles from town, and the local committee built a wooden floor for the tent so that they could have a dance there every night after the show. People came from miles around and we played to capacity. During the week three men came over from Coatsburg, a village in northern Missouri, and said they also were planning a fox hunt and wanted us. We happily signed up with them and played two or three other Iowa towns in the interim. The week before we were to jump to Coatsburg our advance agent called me by telephone and told me nobody in town knew anything about a fox hunt. I rushed down to Coatsburg to see the chairman of the committee. He assured me the hunt would be held as planned and on Sunday we moved the outfit to the designated place— down a dirt road behind a country schoolhouse. When we got there we found out there would not be a fox hunt after all. It then was too late to book another town so we set up the tent. The committee never quite explained what had happened but, recognizing their responsibility for our situation, they did install a Delco light plant for us without charge. We expected a dismal week but about sundown Monday people began to come—they just seemed to materialize out of the woods—and we stood them out every night.

Flushed with that success, I traded the old Dodge in on a brand-new four-cylinder, two-door Chevrolet sedan. If someone today should give us a gold-plated Rolls Royce we would not be half as proud of it as we were of that little car.

During the fall while we were playing a string of house dates I read in a newspaper that an old friend, Alexander Frank of Waterloo, had been placed in charge of the Universal chain of motion picture houses in Iowa. The company had a lease on the old Odeon Opera House in Marshalltown and had boarded it up to eliminate competition. I wired Frank an offer to sublease the Odeon for a stock run and, to my surprise, he let me have it. The contract gave us the customary percentage of the gate but provided that Universal could cancel on two weeks' notice any time that the receipts fell below twelve hundred dollars a week. The Odeon had not had a show for years and dust was inches thick all over the place but we got it cleaned up after a fashion and opened on Christmas Day with *Why Girls Walk Home*. From the start we played to near capacity audiences and soon the movie houses began to hurt. When the Odeon's furnace went on the blink, Universal's local manager refused to repair it but the people still kept coming, even when they had to wear their overcoats and gloves to keep warm. Finally weather got so cold that even the diehards had to give up. Receipts dropped below twelve hundred and we had to close after fourteen weeks.

That was a great turning point for us. One day during the sixth or seventh week I spread ten one-hundred-dollar bills on the bed in our hotel room just to admire them. It was the first time in my life that I ever had so much money at one time. When the engagement ended we had cleared nine thousand dollars. Caroline and I opened an account in the Valley National Bank in Des Moines and had a checkbook printed with our names on it. I felt richer than creosote.

In all my years in repertoire I never knew of a partnership between actors that endured very long. The Schaffner-Lanshaw partnership lasted longer than most—more than two years—but tensions inevitably developed between us. George wanted to make the show more of a dramatic order and to feature Louise. I naturally wanted to make it predominantly a Toby show and argued that the strong line of Toby plays during the 1927 and 1928 tent seasons was the main reason for our increasing success. The argument continued as we began the house tour in the fall of 1928 and so I told George I wanted out. I think he was as relieved as I was.

We gave notice to the cast while we were playing at the Graham Theater in Washington, a bustling little county seat in eastern Iowa. We had made the booking because of a local celebration but when we got to town we discovered that we were faced with an enormous amount of competition from free street attractions. Shortly before show time on our opening night I learned that the first thing on the evening's program was a march around the square by the local militia, led by the town band. The parade route passed right in front of the theater, so when the parade started I fell in behind the militia, carrying a megaphone.

"Now the next big attraction is right down the street," I cried. "Just follow the band! Next big attraction, right down the street —follow the band!"

I did not say free attraction, of course—just big—and a large crowd followed along. George Lanshaw and the house manager stood on the sidewalk and as the crowd approached they just pointed the way into the theater. In a few minutes people were packed in the lobby so tightly that they almost had to buy a ticket so we packed the house that night, but it was our only profitable night on the week.

When we paid off the actors and settled accounts with George, Caroline and I went into Fort Dodge and organized an excellent little seven-people show and played several towns in northern Iowa before moving over into Nebraska to play Crete and Beatrice, where we stayed four weeks. By some wizardry our advance man persuaded the movie chain to let us back into the Odeon Theater in Marshalltown for opening on Christmas Day. With visions of riches before us we enlarged the company to eleven people but somehow the fuzz was off the Marshalltown peach. We never lost money but we did not make any either and when we got a chance to play a week in the beautiful new Circle Theater in Nevada, Iowa, we closed after eight weeks. Nevada was a big winner—a gross of about four thousand dollars—and from that point onward we did excellent business in week stands. Among the houses we played during the spring was the Princess in Fort Dodge, and we had a big week there too. While we were in Marshalltown I had mimeographed the script of *Why Girls Walk Home* and by the time we started rehearsals for the tent season I had leased it to a hundred companies at thirty dollars apiece.

During the winter I learned that Rusty Owens, manager of the Grand Opera House in Ottumwa had acquired a lovely new tent and equipment that had been built especially for Don and Mazie Dixon, who had been highly successful in house repertoire but after one season had all of tent rep they wanted. Rusty was an old friend and he sold us the whole kit and kaboodle— new tent, new chairs and everything—for two thousand dollars. We paid five hundred down and promised to pay off the balance at seventy-five dollars a week. As part of the deal, Rusty agreed to do our advance work for a third of the profits.

Rusty was a native of Ottumwa and had spent most of his life there. In his earlier years he had pitched for the Cleveland Indians and the Chicago White Sox, being one of the heavy-hitting pitchers of his time. As a boy, he also had worked around the Grand Opera House in Ottumwa and on the Jersey Comedy Company, a tent rep show that was owned by the same man, and after retiring from baseball took over the Opera House as manager. He knew a great deal about show business and had friends everywhere. His spectacular job out in front of us, coupled with the beautiful new tent and the fact that we had an excellent show and a strong repertoire of plays, produced an enormously profitable summer.

During the winter I had finished two new plays, *Be Yourself* and *Chain Stores*, both of which we introduced during our opening week at Melcher, Iowa. *Chain Stores* created an immense amount of word-of-mouth advertising and newspaper comment. The whole country was talking then about a radio program over KWKH in Shreveport, Louisiana, called "Hello World," on which a man named W. K. Henderson fulminated nightly against the merchandising chains. Most people came to see *Chain Stores*, I suppose, expecting a sensational exposé. What they got was a darned good evening's entertainment. Joe Whittaker described it in the Marshalltown *Times-Republican* this way:

> The managers of the chain stores thought it favored them. The independent merchants thought it favored them. So everyone was happy, including the audience—which ate it up.

Before the summer was out we had paid for the new outfit in full. Late in September we stored the tent and equipment in the Grand Opera House and played a week there. Then Rusty booked us into Oskaloosa, Grinnell, Centerville, Perry, Sheldon and several other towns and we played to big crowds everywhere. I bought a chocolate-brown 1929 Hudson Big Six sedan with a spare tire on each running board and had "The Schaffner Players" painted on each tire cover in fancy gold leaf. We closed (this time by choice) the week after Thanksgiving and took the entire cast into Kansas City with us. The five acting men had started dressing alike in dark blue overcoats and black derbies and when we hit Kansas City, *Bill Bruno's Bulletin,* a popular tent rep trade journal, observed that The Schaffner Players were "the best dressed show in town."

5

Word of our success preceded us. On the glass door leading to his office in the Gayety Theater Building a dramatic agent, Karl Simpson, listed the more important tent repertoire managers for whom he furnished talent. All of the big ones were there: Doug Morgan, Paul English, Horace Murphy, Jack Brooks, Edgar Jones, Harley Sadler, Hazel Cass, Dubinsky Bros., W. I. Swain, Ed C. Nutt, Skeeter Kell, Roberson & Gifford, Wallace Bruce, Ed Ward, George Sweet and others. One morning I dropped by Simpson's office and at the bottom of the list, in brand-new gold leaf, there was a new name: Neil E. Schaffner.

Kansas City had become the winter gathering place for everybody who was anybody in tent rep. From Thanksgiving to Easter the town was full of managers looking for actors and actors looking for managers and most of them congregated at the Gladstone Hotel. The managers' sanctum was the Round Table in the Gladstone dining doom and I spent many delightful hours there. There was general agreement among all present that a repertoire manager was the most versatile of all people. He managed his show, did the advance work, led his band, directed the orchestra, played the comedy parts and in his spare time acted as boss canvasman. He was businessman, politician, and diplomat, with an astounding capacity for appearing prosperous in just the right degree—enough to convince people in the small towns he played that he was not a fly-by-nighter, but not so well off to arouse suspicion that he was taking too much money out of town.

Hard luck plagued some people, it was agreed, but it always was someone else—never those gathered around the Round Table. Like poor old Oscar V. Howland, the famous tent repertoire character man, who chose to leave his priceless wardrobe at the station overnight when he joined a company in Nebraska on its closing night and the station burned down. Or Willard Collins, who made a hapless matrimonial choice—marrying a town girl who, thinking she was doing something wonderful for Bill, had all his wonderful old clothes cleaned and mended and all the run-down old boots repaired and shined. Or the man named Cook in South Carolina who, having long suffered from insufficient box office, assembled his cast in their Sunday best and solemnly buried a tent stake on the lot, declaring: "I always said that when I reached the a-hole of creation, I would bury a stake in it." If on occasion one of those at the Round Table admitted to some personal miscalculation, he always made it much worse than it actually was.

"We encountered every sort of weather, from the balmiest near-blizzards to the most beautiful floods," said Neale Helvey, describing a foray into East Texas. "When it didn't rain it was getting ready to pour down. During the last week in Lufkin, two of our members froze their ears on one day and two canvasmen were drowned on the lot the following day."

Once in a very great while a manager confessed to a great promotional idea that backfired. Ed Ward said he was touring Kansas with a tent repertoire company that had a brass band. To advertise the show, the band played daily street concerts in the surrounding towns and one of its feature numbers was "Oh You Beautiful Doll" with a vocal refrain. The singer would put the name of each town in the lyrics, singing, "Oh you beautiful Lawrence, you great big beautiful Lawrence," and so on.

"We got along very well," said Ed, "until we got to Pratt."

While great rivalry existed between some tent showmen, the way they told it around the Round Table all were the most honorable of gentlemen and scrupulously refrained from encroaching on one another's territories. There was one famous exception—the contention between J. Doug and Hila Morgan. Hila was the widow of Doug's brother; the two shows generally traveled the same territory and often played the same towns, so there was no love lost between them. If Doug got into a town first and put up his paper, Hila often followed right behind him, plastering the J. Doug Morgan paper with streamers that cried, WAIT FOR HILA, and once Hila's advance man actually stuck one of her streamers on the back of Doug's calliope as it was making its bally through town.

Competition between tent showmen and the managers of local motion picture houses was of another sort. After W. I. "Cap" Swain got his paper up in one Louisiana town the manager of the picture house took out a big ad in the newspaper announcing that during Swain's week everyone would be admitted to the movies free "as an expression of appreciation" for the fine patronage he had enjoyed throughout the year. Cap quietly booked another town for that week and on the day before his opening took out a bigger ad in the newspaper, announcing cancellations of his date—leaving the movie man with a free show on his hands. Jack King, a popular Toby comedian who toured several southeastern states, was having a running fight with a movie house manager in one of his towns. He sent his advance man in to persuade his rival that they ought to bury the hatchet and work together. If on the week before King's stand the movie man would give out free tickets to the tent show, he said, King

would reciprocate by giving out free tickets to the movie house
while he was in town—giving each an opportunity to develop
new patrons among the other's clientele. The movie man agreed;
King admitted all of the movie patrons free on his front door
but sold nearly all of them a reserved seat at a quarter. The next
week the movie man was confronted by nine thousand free
tickets from the tent show, with nothing extra to sell them.

A collective figment of the Round Table's imagination was
Windy Van Hooten. He had a rubber tent that could be ex-
panded to fit any crowd, plus a device that stretched the tent
and released it suddenly, sending it flying from one stand to the
next. Windy constructed his stage and tent poles out of balsa
wood so that the entire outfit could be pedaled from town to
town by canvasmen on bicycles. He also had a glass center pole
with goldfish swimming around in it. At each session Windy's
exploits became more preposterous.

The Gladstone was a paradise for actors' and managers'
dreams as well as their boasts and the air always was full of reports about new shows forming. In three successive issues of
Billboard a new company was reported as forming "to invade
Kansas," as being "in rehearsal for their annual tour of Kansas,"
and as leaving "to play their old established route in Kansas."
In three weeks the show had progressed from a plan to an old
established company. "We made a tremendous effort this week
to get out the *Bulletin* before a certain show which we were announcing as opening on Monday would close," wrote Bill Bruno.
"Unfortunately, we failed by two days." Embellishing success
was a game that everybody played. Rainy days early in the
season were the bane of tent show life but Ed Ward said he
never had that kind of trouble; in fact, in the spring he did better
business when it rained than when it didn't. At that Edgar Jones,
a veteran of many seasons under canvas, got up from the table.
"Well, so long, Ed," he said, "...and a long and rainy season
to you."

I maintained there was not a heavy man in the business who did not aspire to be a Toby comedian and who, against the day when he would be called upon to play the part, did not carry a red wig in his trunk. To prove the point, one day I hailed one of the well-known heavies in the Gladstone dining room and told him I had been asked to do a Toby part in a local show but did not have my wig.

"May I borrow yours?" I asked.

"Sure," he replied, "I'll go right up and get it."

Caroline and I had an incredibly wonderful time in Kansas City that winter. We bought a new fourteen-thousand-dollar home and I felt so flush that I leased *The Family Upstairs* and *Some Baby*, two New York plays, at a hundred and fifty dollars each for the 1930 season. This was much more than repertoire shows ordinarily paid for a play. During the entire winter there was only one little sad note. Caroline and I caught a burlesque show one night and there in the cast was Cecil. I did not make my presence known.

PART FOUR

Overture

———◆———

Overture

1

THE SHOW WAS COSTING NINE HUNDRED DOLLARS A WEEK BUT everything was going swimmingly for us. In the corn and cattle country of southeastern Iowa crops were in excellent shape and we had a bang-up Fourth of July week in Ollie. As Caroline and I drove happily toward Fairfield on Sunday, July 6, 1930, we speculated on what a whopper we ought to have there. Fairfield had about six thousand population. It was an excellent town, with several factories, and it always had been good to us. We were so optimistic that we asked Rusty Owens to come over from Ottumwa and open a second box office for Monday night, our ladies-free night. But on Monday Fairfield stopped dead. We took in exactly thirty dollars, and our gross for the week was barely two hundred.

On the following Sunday, as soon as the outfit was on the road to the next town, Caroline and I drove seventy miles up to Belle Plaine, where the J. Doug Morgan show was playing, and Doug recounted the same astounding experience. His business had been fine right through the Fourth of July, then just dried up, and the week that followed was the worst in the history of his show.

To this day I do not understand how the Depression could have arrived so suddenly. Things went to pot all at once and all over; in towns where we had taken in thirteen hundred dollars the year before we did good to reach three hundred. During the first week of August I called the company together and told them that there no longer was an alternative: I had to cut salaries in half—to $22.50 a week. I offered to honor the Equity contract and give any of them who wanted it two weeks' notice at full salary but none asked for it. By then none of the tent shows was paying any better, if at all.

Like all other tent repertoire shows, we sold advertising banners which were displayed around our proscenium and, strangely, this business held up—producing a hundred dollars or more a week—until we reached Chariton early in August. My first call there was at a hardware store where the owner always had been a strong booster of the show. He turned me down flat.

"Neil," he said, "I don't want any more business. Half of the county owes me money now."

His comment nearly floored me. I stumbled to a bench in front of a grocery store across the street and sat down. For a while I was just blank, but then it occurred to me that the merchants and the Schaffners were in exactly the same fix. What we both needed was cash; that being the case, there ought to be a way we could work together. How? On sudden inspiration, I went up the street to call on another good customer, the owner of a general merchandise store. He was as despondent as the hardware man but it seemed to do him good just to tell somebody about all his unpaid accounts.

"Suppose I could collect a bunch of those back accounts," I said, "would you be willing to pay me twenty percent of what I collect?"

"Brother, and how!" he said. "I'd be tickled to death."

"Well, I'll tell you what I'll do," I said. "I'll buy an ad in the paper and say that I'll give one season pass to The Schaffner Players—good for every night of the week—for every five dollars that is paid on a bill at your store that is more than thirty days old. You pay me a dollar for every ticket you give away. You don't have to invest a cent—we'll settle up at the end of the week."

"I'll do it," he said.

On the strength of his participation, I sold several other merchants on the scheme and we played to the biggest houses in several weeks. We also did well on the reserved seats at ten cents and sold a fair amount of candy. Thereafter we worked some kind of a promotional gimmick in every town. In several places we mailed free season tickets to every rural mailbox, to be honored on the condition that the holder was accompanied by a paying customer. In others we went to the telephone office and, in return for a couple season passes for each of the operators, called all of the rural party lines at once. As people answered the phones I came on and made a spiel that went something like this:

> This is Tobias T. Tolliver talking to you now. I want to tell you about the big tent show tonight, where The Schaffner Players will be putting on a very funny comedy. I have a very good part in that. As a special inducement to all of our friends who live out in the country and are listening to me now, if you come to the big tent tonight and tell the lady at the box office that you came from out in the country, she will let you ladies in free, and your husbands will be admitted to the tent at the same price that others pay.

In Coon Rapids, Iowa, a storm came up on opening night as the curtain was going up on the third act of *The Family Upstairs*. We had to halt the performance but I announced that we would do the last act of the play before starting the Tuesday night show. On Tuesday night another storm came up in the third act of *Chain Stores* and I repeated the offer. We did not get to do a complete show until Thursday night but our method of making good created a favorable impression and we ended up with a fairly good week—and this in spite of the fact that the local movie manager was admitting entire families for forty cents. Such stunts staved off disaster but we nevertheless failed to meet expenses many weeks. It seemed that nearly everybody was in the position of the old Negro that Doug Morgan told me about.

"How much do it cost to git in that show, cap'n?" the old man asked.

"Fifty cents," said Doug.

"How much do you say?"

"Fifty cents."

"Well," said the old man, talking very slowly, "don't depend on me."

Every issue of *Bill Bruno's Bulletin* contained news of early tent shows closings. In each issue, Bruno declared that while it had been a tough season "there is no reason to become panicky." In the September 25 issue, this notice appeared at the bottom of Bruno's editorial column:

> "Wanted—Character man with $2,000 cash; Advance Man with full line of printing; Stage Manager who has outfit of scenery; Director with repertoire of high-class scripts; and people in all lines who have cars. Prefer Juvenile Team with two trucks. Would also like to hear from Comedian with complete tent outfit. Character Man wire. Pay your own. Others write. W. HANK BRUNO.

With that issue, the *Bulletin* suspended publication "until further notice." It did not appear again for four long years.

We closed the tent season at Floris after again playing the fox hunt, to a fraction of the crowds that greeted us a year earlier, and then toured houses until poor business forced us to close at Thanksgiving. We went into Kansas City and there I found the other tent show managers were as numb as we were; with the exception of a few who had shows in Wisconsin they all reported big losses for the season. By Christmas nearly all the money we had made in 1928 and 1929 had drained away but I picked up a little cash by leasing scripts to managers who were able to scrape up twenty-five dollars for the season.

Our first booking in 1931 was the Rialto Theater in Sioux City for a two-bill-a-week stock date beginning New Year's Day. Because Sioux City had a reputation as a good stock town I signed up an all-Equity cast and put salaries up to forty-five dollars a week. Two weeks later I had to cut them back to $22.50. After a fairly good opening, business just kept on sagging and we were saved from disbanding the company only by a timely offer from the President, the big stock and road-show house in Des Moines.

A year or so earlier while we were on our winter tour we had put on one play in the President at the state convention of the Clover Leaf Stores and it made such a hit that the manager of the theater asked me if I thought our show, featuring Toby, would go over as a stock attraction. I naturally told him I thought it would; I had thought so ever since 1925 when I vainly tried to persuade Clyde Gordonier to adopt a Toby policy during our unsuccessful run in Des Moines. At the time of the convention, though, the President did not have an opening for us and we could not have taken it anyway because we were booked solid. Unfortunately, by the time we got there in 1931 the Hatcher Players already had been at the President briefly and the novelty of the Toby idea had worn off. We had tough sledding, but we had an excellent cast and a lot of vaudeville and we managed to hold our head above water. Much of the credit was due Roi Lorenzo.

Roi, who was known far and wide as Nuts Lorenzo, was one of the most eccentric geniuses repertoire ever produced. He could stop anybody's show playing "The World is Waiting for the Sunrise" on the banjo—I think he was every bit as good as Eddy Peabody and some of the other fellows who became famous—and he also was one of the best scenic artists in the business. He could build more for less cost than anybody I ever knew. In Des Moines he promoted a deal with the Younkers Department Store to borrow from their warehouse anything he needed to dress our stage and we put up a string of very fine productions. We received excellent reviews in the Des Moines newspapers.

Absolutely the worst times of the year in show business are the weeks before Christmas and Easter. Since we could not stand much less than we were doing, I began announcing three weeks in advance that during Holy Week we would produce "that great old temperance drama, *Ten Nights in a Barroom*, just as it was first done in 1847." I stressed that it would be "exactly like the show that thrilled your fathers and grandfathers." I did not have a script of the play among my things but Milo Bennett, a booking agent in Chicago, sent one out. I was busy when it arrived and just tossed it on top of one of my trunks and gave it no more thought until time came for rehearsal on Monday before our opening. When the company had gathered, I broke open Bennett's package and to my consternation found that it was a horrible modernized version, set in a soda fountain. I called off rehearsal and telephoned and wired all over the country trying to locate an original script. Bob Sherman, a play broker in Chicago, finally found one but it did not arrive until about noon on Saturday. We had advertised the opening for Sunday matinee so heavily that we had no choice, we had to go on. We read the play through Saturday afternoon, rehearsed it once, parts in hand, on Sunday morning and before the first act that afternoon I went out and made a curtain talk.

> You know, folks, that I have been announcing we would put on this play, *Ten Nights in a Barroom*, just as it was performed back in 1847. Now, at that time, the actors did not memorize their lines as they do today. They had a prompter—a person who sat in a specially-constructed box just below the footlights, following the script and calling

the lines out to them. The actors just repeated the lines
fed them by the prompter. Unfortunately, this theater
does not have a prompt box, so we are going to have our
prompter sit at a table over on the side of the stage where
you can see him. He will be a part of the show, so to speak,
but he will throw the lines and the actors will repeat them
just as it was done in 1847. Now for your enjoyment, The
Schaffner Players present the original version of that great
American classic, *Ten Nights in a Barroom!*

The show was a big hit. The *Register* praised it as one of the
most interesting performances ever seen in Des Moines and
added that the cast "acted as though they really didn't know
the lines."

In our cast at the President we had Eddie Wilson, who played
saxophone and did singing specialties; George Norris, a tall, dark,
handsome man who played a hot trumpet; Harry Goldie, a tall,
dark-haired native of Russia who was a great yodeler and who
also played the ukulele; Pearl Wilson, Harry Goldie's wife and
former wife of Fred Wilson; Eleanor McCracken, a beautiful
lady who had been ingenue on Ed Ward's Princess Stock Company; Bob LaThey, an old-timer in repertoire; and Gladys
Adams, pianist and orchestra leader—all of them seasoned
troupers and excellent actors. We finished up the spring going
strong and I figured that with a company like that I could put
salaries back up to forty dollars when we got under the tent for
the 1931 season. Just before we opened George Norris came to
me and said he had an offer of forty-five a week on another
show down South and I would have to match it or he would
leave. I matched it. Caroline was furious with me. She said that
word would get around and we would have to pay everybody
the same. She was right. Within a few days we had to raise all
salaries to forty-five—and Norris left us anyway.

When we got out into the small towns we discovered that the
Depression really had begun to settle in. We had to cut salaries

back after the first week and it quickly became apparent that the
only way we could keep going was to find some place where
people had money to spend. The bright spot in the Middle West
right then was Ottumwa. The Morrell Packing Company was
packing cheap pork and other meats for export and had about
ten thousand people on its payroll. Wages were low but people
there had more money to spend than almost anywhere else
around so, with Rusty Owens's help, we arranged to set the tent
up on a beautiful lot a few blocks south of the Ottumwa business district. We laid plans for an extended stock engagement
and I spent a great deal of extra money on window cards and
other advertising. When the tent went up on Sunday we had
high hopes. Monday night was just lovely but when we opened
the doors at 7 P.M. not more than a dozen people were out front,
and most of them were comps. I walked across the street to a
city park and sat on a bench trying to wish them in, but as curtain time approached only a few stragglers arrived. Never in my
life was I heavier of heart than when I went backstage and
started putting on my makeup, but I went out and worked my
head off trying to be funny, hoping that the few who had come
would like us enough to go out and tell their friends. But as the
week wore on we played only to a pitiful handful of people.
Those who came seemed to enjoy the show but we were making
no impression at all on the town. At the end of the week
Caroline, Rusty and I sat up practically all one night trying to
figure out what to do. We finally decided we had no choice but
to cut the show way down and to go out and try the very small
towns. The next morning I called the company together and
sorrowfully told them what we had to do and I gave out nine
two-week notices. In spite of that blockbuster, the cast gave a
superlative performance that night and it had an electric effect
on me. When Caroline, Rusty and I got together after the show
as usual, I told them I was determined to stay in Ottumwa.

"How do the people of Ottumwa know they don't like this

show?" I asked. "Not enough of them have seen it. I'm going to get them in here somehow if I have to let them in free!"

"I'm not willing to go *that* far," said Caroline.

Again we sat up into the small hours, discarding one idea after another, and finally I remembered having read an ad in the Des Moines paper about public-address systems for sale. Before going to bed, I wrote the concern and asked whether their equipment could be installed in my automobile and what it would cost. They replied that it could be installed in the car for ninety dollars. That took practically the last cent we had but one night after the show Bob LaThey and I drove to Des Moines and as soon as the store opened I bought the outfit and they started installing it. The main works, which operated off the car battery, came in a sort of motoring trunk, which they installed in the back seat of the Hudson. There was a turntable on top of the trunk, a microphone and two loudspeakers, which were installed in the back windows after the glass had been removed. When the installation was completed, Bob and I set out for Ottumwa, arriving in time to take one turn around the main streets of town. I announced over the loudspeaker that "all ladies are free tonight at the big tent theater ... absolutely no strings attached ... all ladies free tonight at the big tent theater." Between my announcements Bob played records, turning the volume way up. Here and there people came out of their houses to see what the racket was and I grabbed the microphone and made my spiel. That night a sizeable number of women but very few men were on hand, but we took in about sixty dollars, which was more than twice what we had been doing.

The next day was Saturday and Bob and I spent practically the whole day traversing the town, making side streets as well as all of the main thoroughfares, and that night a few more men came along with the women. Our receipts jumped to nearly a hundred dollars. On Sunday I met with the actors who had been given notices and told them I would keep them on if they were willing to stay on a week-to-week basis, without the customary notice. They all stayed.

During our third week receipts rose to about a hundred and seventy-five dollars a day and I decided to go all out for volume. We had been charging thirty-five cents for adults and fifteen cents for children on the front door, plus a dime for reserved chairs. During the later part of the week I announced both from the stage and from the loudspeaker as we toured the town that on Sunday we would admit ladies free and cut the price for men to a dime. That meant that a man and his wife could buy reserved seats and still see the show for a total of thirty cents. People began to come in such numbers that I had to get an extra middle for the tent. We kept adding chairs until we had sixteen hundred, plus the blues in the back. By this time we were wrecking the movie houses. I heard that on one night the Capital, the ace house in town, played to a gross of only seven dollars. The local manager for one of the movie chains complained to the mayor and as a result the city clerk wrote me a note saying that after the current week my licenses could not be extended. That night before the show I stepped out on the orchestra platform, took off my red wig and made a speech.

> Ladies and gentlemen, it is very seldom that I ever make a serious talk, as you know, but now an occasion has arisen that makes it necessary for me to talk sensibly to you. As you know, we came into Ottumwa some three or four weeks ago and the crowds were very small. And then crowds began to swell, getting larger and larger each night as you people came to see our plays. Now certain interests in Ottumwa, whose only concern with the town is the money they can take out of it, to send out to Hollywood for million-dollar liquor parties and divorce suits, have gone to your mayor and council and have complained about us. Your city clerk has served notice on me that we will be granted no more licenses after this week.... Now your very presence in this theater tonight is evidence to me that you are at least in some degree interested in the

spoken stage and its preservation. The Schaffner Players have never been run out of any place and we do not intend to be run out of Ottumwa. . . . Friends, on the first day of February 1919, my Uncle Sam took me by the hand and said, "You have served your country in her hour of need; now go and earn your living and care for your loved ones." The only thing on God's green earth I have to sell is my ability as an entertainer but now they say I shan't even be allowed to do that. Now, if you people, as taxpayers and voters in Ottumwa, have a right to select your own entertainment and not be dictated to by Hollywood, then call your mayor and council and inform them of that fact. They are your servants. They are working for you and I am sure they want to do what you want them to do, so if you want The Schaffner Players to remain in Ottumwa, tell that to your mayor and your city council.

Next day more than two thousand telephone calls poured into the city hall. One woman said it took her more than five hours to get through. When she finally reached the mayor she told him, "You better not run for office again if you chase that tent show out of town." About six o'clock the city clerk called Rusty.

"Get those women off of us!" he pleaded. "We can't do anything. That tent show can have a license from now to eternity as far as we are concerned, but get those women off."

2

After Labor Day we jumped the tent down to Derby, Iowa, for a banner week at the fair, then moved the show into the Grand Opera House, a beautiful old theater seating about eight hundred.

We gave ten performances a week—one show each night Monday through Friday, a matinee and one night show on Saturday and a matinee and two evening performances on Sunday—and charged twenty cents for reserved seats on the main floor and a dime for the balconies. Soon we were sold out three or four days in advance and many people made permanent reservations for the opening of each new play (Monday and Friday). Our business became the talk of the Middle West; no one else in show business could understand it. The answer was simple: we had so much show at such a low price that people just could not stay away. The chain movie houses became so desperate that the Ottumwa Theater, which had a big stage, put in five acts of vaudeville to buck us. The opening bill featured Dave Vine, a big-time vaudeville entertainer whom I had known when trouping with Bert Rose, and the day before his opening I invited him and all the other acts to visit our show. When they arrived I told our audience that we were very proud to have some famous vaudeville entertainers visiting us backstage and introduced each of the acts. When Dave Vine came out I started doing a gag act with him and he went along with the fun. Next day a notice went up backstage at the Ottumwa that no performer was to appear in any other theater while in town.

The Ottumwa's vaudeville policy lasted only a few weeks; the public could not see paying fifty cents to see five acts of vaudeville and a movie when they could come to the Grand and for twenty cents see not only four acts of vaudeville but a three-act play and a stage presentation by a ten-piece orchestra as well. In midwinter the movie people again went to the mayor and complained about the competition we were giving him. This time the mayor was unmoved.

"I know you have a hard time explaining to your bosses in New York and Hollywood how this farmer boy with a three-dollar red wig, down the back alley, is licking you with your million-dollar stars," he said, "but the fact is he is and I can't do anything about it. The public wants that show and that's all there is to it."

Doing two bills a week was no particular trick for a bunch of seasoned troupers like we had, and by leasing an occasional play like *Mrs. Wiggs of the Cabbage Patch*, *The Gorilla* or *Daddy Longlegs* we had plenty of material, but we all soon began to run dry on fresh material for specialties. Fairly early in the fall we started hiring vaudeville people as "extra added attractions." One day we had just finished rehearsal when the stage door opened and in stumbled the toughest-looking little mug I ever saw outside of a gangster movie. He was short, bow-legged and dirty and had not shaved for several days. Talking out of the side of his mouth, he asked if I could use a good song and dance man. I told him no.

"Well, I am going to do an audition up at the radio station at noon," he said, "so tune in."

During lunch, more or less from habit, I turned on the radio and out of it came one of the most beautiful voices I have ever heard. It was like molten gold; it just flowed. Then the announcer came on and said, "That was Billy Stone, the Rolling Stone of the Air, making his initial appearance on our station." I called Doug Grant, the program director at the station, and asked him to describe the man I had just heard singing. Billy Stone and the tramp were one and the same, so I asked Grant to have Stone come back. We put him on that night and eyes bugged out all over the house when he started to sing. The people of Ottumwa took him to their hearts and he built an enormous following. One night we did an Indian presentation before the play and he stood on a rock and sang "Indian Love Call." When he came off I complimented him and in a matter-of-fact way he said, "Yes, Publix paid me two hundred and seventy-five dollars a week last winter to sing that song." I was paying him fifteen.

Billy was enormously talented. Not only could he put over almost any kind of song but he also played drums and was a terrific tap dancer. He had one routine I never saw anyone else do—bouncing from feet to hands and from floor to piano stool without missing a beat. He stayed with us until the day after

Christmas and then just disappeared. I never heard of him again until the early forties, when I ran into him on the street in Chicago. He had a small orchestra there.

Another unusual character came to the apartment one day and announced himself as Buddy Ballinger, the king of the mouth harp. He said he had worked in a motion picture short out in Hollywood and was on his way back East but had run out of money. He was trying to get to Burlington, where he had a friend who would advance him funds for the rest of the trip, and asked me to use him just one night.

"If I go out there and don't stop your show it won't cost you a cent," he said. "But if I do stop your show, will you give me two dollars to buy enough gas to get on to Burlington?"

We put him on and I never heard anyone get so much music out of a harmonica. He tied the show in knots. I gave him two dollars and he went happily on his way.

By spring we had done about a hundred and seventy-five plays. I had written several new ones and had doctored practically all the old scripts in my trunk. I even rewrote *Man of Mystery*, in which I had appeared with Spedden & Paige in 1909 —making a Toby out of the original blackface part. In the spring, more or less in desperation, I fixed up the old-time play *Tennessee's Partner* by writing a prologue and an epilogue and putting on the whole thing as it was written. In the prologue, the landlord of a hotel is standing behind the desk when two young men in golfing attire come in. One of them mentions that while out on the golf course he had seen a bronze plate bearing the name Asa Bice and asks if there is a story behind it.

"Well, yes," says the landlord. "It was forty years ago when one of my boarders, a man named Barlow, was sitting at that very table over there and. . . ."

The lights dim down and out, the two young fellows exit and

the Barlow character takes his place at the table. The lights come up and the play proceeds. At the last line the lights dim down and out again, the golfers come on and as the lights come back up they thank the landlord for such an interesting story. End of show. It was received amazingly well.

By the time we did *Tennessee's Partner* all of us were studied out. Between directing, doing comedy and specialties, rewriting and updating old plays and every Monday night after the show driving up to Fort Dodge to see my mother, who became very ill, I had grown tired both physically and mentally. I began to think that if the people in Ottumwa liked our show so much the county seats on the road would do the same, so in April we started out on a week-stand repertoire tour.

The county seats were not overjoyed to see us but at least we got some rest and, except for Buddy and Corrinne Williams, a featured dancing act in our vaudeville, the company remained intact. Because of their spectacular dance routines, the Williamses had been an asset at the Grand and Corrinne had been a pleasant addition to the acting cast as well. Buddy was such an untalented actor, though, that we gave him parts only when we absolutely had to. Before joining us the Williamses had gone without salaries for some time on another show and Buddy once told me that if they had not been able to give some dancing lessons on the side they actually would have gone hungry. Along in the spring he proudly showed me a hundred-dollar bill they had saved and told me, as he had many times, how grateful he was for the chance of working for us. But during the first week of our repertoire tour he gave notice. He said he was unhappy about the parts I was giving him and he and Corrinne were going back on the show they had left because of unpaid salary.

"He'll let me play leads," he said.

Even in midsummer when green fields of corn reach out for miles around it, Marshalltown looks like an oasis. There are so

many trees that as you approach it you have a feeling of coming
upon an immense arboretum. Only the friendly clock tower of
the courthouse and the smokestacks of the factories reveal that
a town lies ahead. It is a deceptive view. Instead of a languid
village, Marshalltown turns out to be an up-and-doing kind of
town. Even at the depths of the Depression this was so, and we
were anxious to get there in the summer of 1932. We thought
surely Marshalltown would give a boost to our sagging fortunes.

When I went in to book the town the city clerk advised me
that the council had passed a new ordinance raising licenses for
tent shows to a hundred and fifty dollars a week, or some such
outrageous figure, but I looked through the ordinance book and
found a provision for an annual amusement park license for
twenty-five dollars. I thanked the clerk and went out to locate
some people I knew about who owned a baseball park that was
not being used at the time. They rented it to us for a small percentage of our gross and I went back and took out an amusement
park license. Word of our little coup leaked out while our tent
was going up and the movie interests raised Holy Ned. Some city
functionary came out to tell me I could not show there. I suggested that the gentleman look up the ordinance, which described "amusement park" in the most general terms.

"So far as I am concerned," I said, "an amusement park is a
place with a fence around it in which amusements are offered.
We qualify because we are offering amusements."

That night the city council was called into a special session
to decide what to do next. Fortunately, the alderman for the
ward in which the baseball park was located was an old friend
and a booster of The Schaffner Players. He blocked action by
the council at that meeting. The next day the Marshalltown
Times-Republican came out with a long story on the front page
relating the main movie interest complaints about us—that we
were a "fly by night outfit," that we "took money out of town"

while they stayed there and paid taxes, and so on. Joe Whitaker, the city editor, came out to see me and said that the columns of his paper were open to me to reply in equal length but that as a friend he would advise me to say nothing at all. I took his advice; that evening there was a front-page box which said, "Neil Schaffner says, 'No Comment.' " The publicity helped our business considerably. A day or two later the head of the local musicians' union dropped by the tent for a visit and I made quite a point of the fact that all of our musicians carried union cards and that all our actors belonged to Equity. The next day the head of the local building trades paid a visit and I repeated the statement for his benefit. Both men went before the council and declared their members would not sit still and let the city officials run a show like ours out of town just to please the movie people, who hired very few union members and no musicians at all. Several other citizens, on their own, also appeared to protest and the council backed down. One of the councilmen came out to the park and asked me what I thought a fair license would be. I helped him work out a formula based on the number of seats in a tent, the admission charge and so on, and the council passed a new ordinance. I suppose it still is on the books.

Some version of the movie-inspired Marshalltown harassment confronted us in practically every town that summer but we finally found a way to put an end to it. A lawyer in Des Moines recalled that at the end of World War I the state legislature had passed a law providing that any ex-serviceman had the right to "hawk, vend, peddle or sell any article of his own manufacture" without any license whatever. When the mayor of Osceola told me that under "discretionary power" granted him by the town ordinances he was raising my licenses to a hundred dollars a week, I called his attention to that law.

"Inasmuch as I wrote all of the plays we are using," I said, "I take the position that I am selling an article of my own manufacture. I am an Iowa ex-serviceman and I am not going to pay any license at all."

"You will be subject to arrest," the mayor said.

"That's just fine with me," I replied. "As a matter of fact, I think I will insist on you arresting me so I can file suit for damages under this state law. We'll see how it comes out."

This seemed to disturb the mayor so I told him I was going out for some lunch and would be back later to see what he intended to do. When I came back he offered me the license at the usual amount and I paid it.

Overt acts by the movie people to stop us actually hurt us much less than the talk they inspired about how the show "took money out of town." This was very effective poison in those days of deep depression. One afternoon I dropped in on one of our good customers, a hardware merchant, and asked if he was coming to the show that night.

"No, I don't think so," he said. "I don't believe in patronizing things like your show that take all the money out of town. Times are too hard."

As I entered the store I had noticed an expensive new car at his curb. I asked if it was his and he said it was.

"Do you realize that more money went out of this town when you bought that car than I'll take out of here in four or five years?" I asked. "As a matter of fact, did you ever stop to think that every item in your stock represents dollars that went out of town? Most of the money I take in stays right here. I have fifteen or twenty people on my show and I pay all of them wages while I'm here, and most of what they get they spend here for lodging, meals, laundry, clothes and other needs. Why, if I played to capacity business every night I'd be lucky to make a profit of twenty percent. In other words, I take a maximum of twenty percent out of town and leave eighty percent. With you, it's just the opposite—you keep twenty percent and send all the rest out of town."

He came to the show that night. Trouble was, though, I couldn't take on every merchant in every town we played.

During the summer of 1932 Caroline and I finally concluded, after much discussion, that if the movies could show on Sunday we could too. We decided to give it a try at Wapello, where we had an unusually loyal following, but I made a mistake and asked the mayor for his approval. He was evasive. I visited with him almost every day during the week but he kept putting me off, so on Friday and Saturday night I took a chance and announced from the stage that we would have a show on Sunday. This provoked no response from His Honor and I assumed we were in the clear, but on Sunday morning the mayor walked up as I was sitting on the front porch of the hotel.

"Pull up your stakes and git!" he said, then turned on his heels and walked off.

We left. In the next town we asked no advice and sought no official approval; we just gave the Sunday night performance a big buildup and did good business. From that time on we played seven days a week, and in time Sunday became one of our biggest nights.

3

From the beginning of The Schaffner Players, we had booked a number of Iowa towns that also were played every year by the J. Doug Morgan Show. Doug and I had become very good friends and every spring we got together to talk over our routes for the summer. If he wanted to go into a town early in the summer I would go in late; if I wanted to go in early he would come in late. The scheme worked very well and we had a number of the better towns pretty much to ourselves. After our big 1929 season I shot off my mouth around the Gladstone Hotel about the tremendous business we had done in New Sharon and among

those who overheard me was Bart Nevious of the Nevious &
Tanner show, which ordinarily trouped in Missouri. In the summer of 1930, Nevious & Tanner played New Sharon ahead of
me. Doug heard about it, went over to see Nevious and told him
that if he ever did that again he would jump the J. Doug Morgan
Show clear across the country, if necessary, and "day and date"
him. Nevious must not have taken him seriously because in 1931
he again booked New Sharon ahead of me and Doug jumped his
show from way down in the southern part of Missouri and set
up his tent right across the street from Nevious & Tanner. Because he had such an elaborate outfit, he naturally snowed
Nevious under. With all this history behind us, I was amazed to
find one day during the summer of 1932 that the Morgan show
had put up paper in Mt. Pleasant, which Doug always had re-
spected as my town. I practically blew my top. Doug was playing Washington that week and I drove right over there, seething
all the way. By the time I got to his lot I was ready to punch him
in the nose but wound up, instead, going into partnership with
him.

Doug had a wonderful string of towns in East Texas that he
played in the fall but he did not have a very good show that year.
I did, so he proposed that we join forces for a fall and winter
tour. When we closed in Iowa I took most of my cast and four
of his people and we played three towns in Missouri and jumped
with his big tent all the way down to Honeygrove, Texas. I had
heard it said that northern Tobies never clicked in the South
because people there were accustomed to the slower-talking
brand of southern humor. But before I went on in Honeygrove,
Doug went out and made a very flowery speech, building me
up big, and the audience gave me a wonderful reception.

Doug had a very colorful show. He advertised it as the J.
Doug Morgan Show in the Big Circus Tent, ballyhooed it with
a calliope and started everything with a whistle. To open every
performance he strode down the center aisle, took a position in

front of the stage and in the manner of a circus ringmaster bellowed in a voice you could hear into the next county, "Welcome to the J. Doug Morgan Show." The outfit was so big that he carried eleven working men, whom he furnished meals in a large semi-trailer truck into which he had built a regular lunch counter, plus a booth for six people at one end. The cook, a burly Negro, had been chef to the governor of Louisiana and prepared some really wonderful meals. Since Doug permitted the actors to buy meal tickets at cost, Caroline and I usually had our meals in the trailer. Doug and his wife, Elsie, customarily ate a little later in the afternoon. One day I happened to drop into the trailer and found the Morgans dining on roast duck. Since we shared expenses and since nothing like that ever had been set before Caroline and me, I was more than a little teed off and said so. Doug responded in kind and we had quite an argument, but then we both let it drop and went on with our work.

We made a little money up until Thanksgiving, when business fell off because of the chilly nights. Then we got into Longview, which was having an oil boom, and our business was so good during the first part of the week that I suggested to Doug that we stay there and play stock for the rest of the winter. He did not want to do that so I told him I thought it was time we parted company. Looking back after all these years, though, I am sure it was nòt that disagreement over policy that did in our partnership. It was that blasted roast duck dinner.

One fine thing came out of that adventure with the Morgan show. Like all other tent shows, we had been giving a concert, or after-show, following the play on Saturday night and while it was going on our canvas crews practically tore the tent down from around the audience. Doug Morgan had such a large working crew that they really made a shambles of the tent while the concert was taking place and after one particularly noisy teardown Caroline said that when we went out with our own show again we were not going to tear down while any part of the show was in progress.

"This is absolutely ridiculous," she said. "Those people pay good money to see the concert and they are entitled to see it, and hear it, without all this confusion. We are just not going to have it."

The idea horrified me; I thought the canvas crews needed to start early in order to get to the next town in time. But as in so many other things across the years, Caroline turned out to be absolutely right; we made the jump just as well by starting the teardown after the concert as during it. Saturday always had been the weakest night on the week but when we stopped the early teardown business began to build. We began using stronger plays and that boosted business still more. When times improved, we started leasing New York farces for Saturday night—among them *Twin Beds, Up in Mabel's Room,* and *Getting Gertie's Garter*—and it became the biggest night of the week. We dropped the concert altogether.

After leaving Doug Morgan in Texas, Caroline and I went back into Kansas City for a little rest and then began to make plans for winter and spring. Rusty Owens had been urging us to come back to Ottumwa but I thought that after our long run there we should leave Ottumwa alone for a year or two. Instead, I booked the Clinton Theater in Clinton, Iowa, hoping for an extended stock run. On our way to Clinton we drove through Ottumwa and I nearly fell out of my seat when we passed the Grand Opera House and saw the sign on the marquee. In small letters it said, "The Goldie-Wilson Players, former stars of" and then in immense letters, "THE SCHAFFNER PLAYERS." I have never been more upset. I stormed into Rusty's office and told him in no uncertain terms he had to take that sign down.

"I don't particularly mind you bringing in another popular price show, even though I urged you not to do it," I said, "but I just cannot stand to have anybody trading on the Schaffner name."

Rusty said he would take the sign down (and he did) but he said I had to understand his side of it. He could not just sit there with an empty house and he had asked Harry Goldie and Eddie Wilson to put together a show and bring it in. They had done so only because he asked them to do it. I cooled down a bit and we shook hands, and Rusty said he still would like us to come back whenever we were ready.

In other circumstances, playing the Clinton Theater would have been a privilege. It was a lovely old building with a brick and red sandstone front, and the traces of the elegance of its earlier days, dating back to 1882, were still to be found inside. Maud Adams, Nora Bayes, Alla Nazimova, John Drew, Otis Skinner, Margaret Anglin and Lillian Russell all had performed there but the glories were in the past; we could not make expenses, so we returned to Ottumwa, hoping to pick up where we had left off at the Grand Opera House. We didn't. The Depression had tightened its grip on Ottumwa, too, and we just existed. The bank holiday in March nearly wrecked us but we had nowhere to go and nothing else to do so we just held on until we could take the tent out again at the middle of May. We did no better on the road.

For some time I had been thinking about Burlington, which had some fairly sizeable payrolls but which had not had a show like ours. When I went over to make arrangements, I discovered that there was a separate corporation called West Burlington, which had a lovely little city park right on the highway. I called on the mayor and made a deal to put my tent there for fifteen dollars a week. For once, the local merchants were pleased as anything to have us because they thought the show might help attract business to West Burlington. Capitalizing on this situation, we worked out a "merchants' plan" under which any merchant who paid a dollar a week for the privilege could have as many free general admission tickets to the show as he wanted to pass out among his customers. A hundred and ten merchants signed up under the plan, and I picked up another five dollars a week by giving the Shultz Baking company the privilege of inserting a free ticket under the wrapper of each loaf of bread it sold. When you consider the circumstances, this was a pretty good deal. We were paying actors fifteen dollars a week and I paid a total of fifteen dollars a week for room and board—and magnificent board it was—for my family of three. At least half of the cooperating merchants bought our advertising banners at five dollars a week and we had about eight hundred reserved chairs to sell at a dime, plus our candy, popcorn and cold drinks. The merchants talked up the show and we opened to excellent attendance, but one afternoon shortly after our opening I was called to the telephone while visiting an old friend in downtown Burlington. A voice I did not at once recognize (it was Roi Lorenzo) asked if I was the man who had the tent show out in West Burlington. I said I was and he said, "You're a liar. It just blew away."

I jumped into my car and raced out to West Burlington and, sure enough, the tent had been riddled by a sudden local storm. Hardly a piece of canvas as big as a handkerchief was left on the ropes. For a while Caroline and I were just numb. We had no idea how or whether we could ever pay for another tent, but the next day a man came down, took measurements and said he could build a duplicate tent for six hundred dollars. I told him to go ahead. That night we put up the sidewalls and played under the ropes. While the new tent was being built we did not lose a single performance because of rain. We stayed in West Burlington thirteen weeks. While there Rome Lee, then seven years old, made his debut as an actor.

I thought it would be a great novelty to have Rome play Toby in one show a week and so I cut an old wig down to fit him and we rehearsed him in *No Wedding Bells*. The night be-

fore he was to go on I gave him a big buildup in my curtain talk
and we had a big crowd for him. He knew all his lines (in fact
he knew the lines of all our plays) and he did very well but his
little child's voice did not carry, so Caroline and I kept calling
to him from the wings to speak up. Long after we had retired
that night Caroline waked me up to listen to him talking in his
sleep.

"You have to talk loud if you want them to hear you. Speak
louder! You have to talk loud. . . ."

He thrashed around all through the night, groaning and re-
peating the words over and over. We did not let him step on the
stage as a performer again until he was sixteen.

We wound up the season at the fair in the little town of Win-
field, where the fair association paid us five hundred dollars flat
for the week. When we had paid off the actors and stored the
tent in Wapello we had about two hundred dollars left. Since my
mother still was very ill, we went into Fort Dodge, put Rome
Lee in the Lincoln School, which was the same one I attended at
his age, and organized a circle stock.

Most circles carried as little in the way of settings and equipment as possible, often using only diamond-dye backdrops, but
we carried practical doors, a trouping ceiling piece, bracket
lights, extra footlights and dimmers and spent a great deal of time
dressing up our stage for every performance. Caroline insisted
on the cast being immaculate and attention to such details paid
off in fine business at the start of the season. Mother passed away
early in October and that left Dad on my hands. He was eighty-
six and after Mother's death he began to fail mentally so we had
to take him with us everywhere we went. One night when we
were playing Luverne it turned bitter cold and on the way back
I gave Dad my overcoat. I got very cold and the next day came
down with pneumonia. They took me to a private hospital,
where they drained five quarts of liquid from my lungs and gave

me a thorough dry-cleaning and pressing job and kept me for five weeks. For many days I was not entirely aware of what was going on around me and one afternoon when I awoke I was shocked to find my brother Rome sitting by my bed. Since he had been down for Mother's funeral six weeks earlier, my first thought was that I was going to die but he said the reason he had come was that Dad had passed away. They already had held the funeral.

Caroline had managed to keep the circle going and when I got on my feet again Lorin Guin joined us and we built up a fair business for the rest of the season. Meanwhile, I spent every available minute at the typewriter and finished two plays, which I leased to enough shows for capital to launch the 1934 tent season. To get around a prohibitive tent show license, we opened at Fort Dodge as an airdome (for which the license was only about twenty dollars)—putting up the sidewalls but not the tent —and after three indifferent weeks there played a bang-up week in Nevada, southeast of Fort Dodge. Then we moved toward our regular territory. While we were playing Burlington, my old friend Skeeter Kell came up for a visit and urged me to take my show south for the winter and this became more and more attractive as the season wore on because we did substantially more business than in 1933. Since my tour with Doug Morgan had proved to me that my brand of comedy would be accepted down there, we decided to go to Texas. In late September we jumped to Canton, Missouri, and from there to Edina. We planned to move on southward in easy jumps but the weather turned bad suddenly and we had such terrible business in Edina that we put the tent in storage there and decided to try circle stock again. We stayed at the Hatfield Hotel in Edina and put Rome Lee in school, in the third grade, and prospered after a fashion until Christmas. Then snow began to fall; the unpaved side roads became impossible to navigate and at once the bottom dropped out of our business. When a friend of mine named

Lester Martin, who had managed the theater in Nevada, offered me a job helping him with a state popularity contest he had developed, we disbanded the circle.

One night early in the year when we dropped into a sandwich shop after the show we saw a very amateurish handbill advertising the "Lone Star Ranger from Kentucky." We had a big laugh about it and when we came back the next week I asked the old gentleman who pulled the curtain at the opera house what the show was like.

"That was the rottenest thing I ever saw but they packed the house twice at thirty-five cents a head," he said. "People thought he was the Lone Ranger they had heard on the radio."

On the way up to handle my first contest for Lester Martin I got to thinking about the "Lone Star Ranger from Kentucky" and stopped in Des Moines for a talk with Irving Grossman, the personnel manager of Radio Station WHO, to see if there was not some way the Schaffners could horn in on the station's popular Saturday night show, the "WHO Barn Dance Frolics." Grossman was cooperative, though we did not come up with anything then, and when Martin's statewide popularity contest scheme fizzled, I proposed that we put on "WHO Barn Dance Frolics" amateur contests in theaters around the state—the winners to be given a spot on the Saturday night show in Des Moines. Grossman agreed to this and the scheme worked fairly well in a few of the large towns but did so poorly in the small ones that I went back to Edina. Caroline, Guin and I played the circle with one-act plays and did quite well until we opened the tent show season. Then we hit bottom again. Our opening week was so bad that the only way I could pay expenses and jump the show to the next town was to float a bank loan, and the only way I could do that was to pledge Caroline's engagement ring as security. So far as I am concerned, that was absolutely the low point of the Schaffners.

I kept hearing reports that a unit of entertainers from the Barn Dance Frolics was pulling big crowds in theaters—grossing five hundred dollars a night while we were doing forty—so I made a deal with the station to take the unit on a summer tour of one nighters under our tent. We played nearly every night in the rain for two or three weeks and packed them in. Then the rain stopped; farmers went back to the fields and our business went with them. Fortunately the Fourth of July soon rolled around and the farmers came back to town. We cleared enough on eight performances at Clear Lake, Iowa, to get Caroline's ring out of hock, pay off the performers and close the Frolics show. We went back to week-stand repertoire and did pretty good business for the rest of the season. One of the things that helped was a four-act play, *Jittering Spooks*, that I had finished during the winter. We gave a free after-show each night—one act of *Spooks* each night for four nights—and it was amazingly potent for pulling them back.

Many months had passed since we had made a payment on the mortgage on our home in Kansas City and just as we were closing the tent for the season the building and loan company foreclosed. We owed only twenty-one hundred dollars, but all we had to our name was six hundred dollars and I could not raise the balance anywhere.

4

One day in September while we were playing West Burlington, Johnny Palmer, the business manager of a 250-watt radio station, WCAZ, in Carthage, Illinois, came there to sell advertising and we got to talking about this radio thing that bothered me. We examined and discarded several ideas for getting Caroline and me on radio but finally a scheme emerged: the Schaffners would go on WCAZ and do a fifteen-minute comedy show five days a week without pay; the station would let us use some air time every day to promote a circle stock out of Carthage and we would split the proceeds with the station. When I told Caroline about it she was aghast.

"What in the world are we going to do for fifteen minutes every day, five days a week?" she asked. "We don't play instruments or anything like that."

"We're going to tell jokes," I said.

"Do you have any idea how many jokes it will take to fill up fifteen minutes five times a week?"

"I don't know," I said, "but it doesn't make any difference. We're going to tell jokes."

Knowing it was not good to keep moving Rome Lee from school to school, we put him in the Roosevelt Military Academy over at Aledo, Illinois. We just barely had enough money to buy his uniforms and pay one month's tuition.

I tried without success to line up several high school auditoriums for the circle and then settled on a couple of theaters and several movie houses and town halls, all of which took a bigger share of our gross. We organized the company and then started our radio show, doing various "Toby & Susie" specialties and skits we had accumulated over the years. The radio show caused considerable talk but, to our surprise, it did not help the circle at all; we barely made expenses. One day by chance Caroline and I put together a bunch of yarns having to do with happenings around a newspaper office and as we came out of the studio the owner of the station stopped us.

"It was pretty good today," he said. "Why don't you develop a skit that is always in the newspaper office?"

We leaped at the idea because already it was getting hard to dig up enough unrelated gags to fill seventy-five minutes of air time every week. While trying to think of a funny name for Toby's newspaper Caroline remembered a road sign in Texas pointing to Bugtussle, so we called it the Bugtussle News. We made it a sort of joking gossip column, sprinkling our gags with

names of people in Carthage and other towns in the WCAZ
area.

> SUSIE: Here's a fan letter I got from Joe Thompson. He
> says, "Dear Susie, you are my dream girl and I am
> enclosing a check for one thousand kisses."
> TOBY: That was real nice. How did you answer?
> SUSIE: I wrote, "Thanks for the check. Jim Johnson
> cashed it."

The show caught on quickly and within a few weeks we
began to get reports that when we were on the air business came
to a standstill all over central and western Illinois. Storekeepers
actually refused to wait on their customers until we were off
the air. Soon we started getting letters from parent-teacher organizations, senior classes and service clubs asking if they could
make arrangements for us to appear in their towns. "Toby &
Susie" quickly outgrew The Schaffner Players. We closed the
circle and started playing personal appearances in school auditoriums and theaters. Our first personal appearance in a regular
theater was at the Columbia in Fort Madison, which we had
played earlier with the circle. We booked in there for a fifteen-
minute vaudeville act between the movies and since Fort Madison was a larger town than Carthage we drove over for Sunday
dinner. We arrived about noon and saw people lined up on one
of the downtown streets, around the corner from the theater.

"My, my, what's going on here?" I asked. "We must have
some terrible competition today."

We ate our dinner and then drove up to the theater. All those
people were waiting to see us! Up on the marquee there was a
big sign, IN PERSON, TOBY & SUSIE, STARS OF TOBY'S
BUGTUSSLE NEWS. When we had played the Columbia on
the circle we felt lucky to get a third of a house, but that day
we packed them to the rafters for three performances.

Bookings suddenly became no problem at all. Now that we
were radio stars, committees came to call on us from some of

the very towns where I had failed to make headway getting auditoriums for the circle. Many nights when I looked out and
saw people lined up for "Toby & Susie," I called out to Caroline,
"I heard them on the radio!" That became a standing gag with
us forever after when a big crowd formed in front of our tent.
In spite of my imprudence in agreeing to split proceeds with the
radio station, we cleared as much as a hundred dollars some
weeks and were able to make some progress in reducing the
enormous debts we had piled up as a result of the "WHO Barn
Dance Frolics" show. There was one period along in February,
though, when bad weather cut down attendance at our public
appearances and Caroline became very discouraged.

"If ever again I have a ten-dollar bill that doesn't belong to
someone else," she said, "I'll be supremely happy."

I told her it was bound to get better.

"Honey, this radio is going to be the big thing," I said. "The
day will come when you will hear the announcer say that Toby
and Susie appeared on this program through the courtesy of
something or other and, 'This is the National Broadcasting Company.' "

Caroline just snorted.

We carried the Toby and Susie idea into the 1936 tent show
by making Susie as big a feature as Toby in most of our plays.
This served a double purpose: it made good on our advertising
of "Toby & Susie—Direct from Radio," and it also made possible
Caroline's escape from the ingenue roles she had played so long.
She felt she was too old for such parts but too young for characters and the Susie part was the perfect answer. The combination of our new radio fame and a first-rate show produced fifty
percent more business than we had done the year before. Everywhere people addressed us as Toby and Susie. Only old personal
friends called us by our real names and even they sometimes
slipped into the Toby and Susie bit.

One of the reasons we had such a good show was an extraordinary character team, Ned and Edna Allen. Reluctantly and bit-by-bit, they told us that their real names were Doone and that for years they had operated a big musical revue that trouped the Far East. When they at last decided to settle in one place they bought a racetrack in Sydney, Australia, and made a great deal of money until a grandstand collapsed, injuring many people. To avoid the ensuing lawsuits, they skipped the country and were waiting out the statute of limitations before returning.

Among my specialties, I was doing a parody of "Where the River Shannon Flows" and one day Ned suggested that the act might be given extra punch if he came on after me and sang the song straight. He could say that he resented the whole thing because he was Irish and the River Shannon was sacred to all Irishmen, and then offer to sing a chorus in the regular way, inviting the audience to express an opinion about which version it liked best. When Ned sang that chorus it was like dropping a bomb in the audience. He had a wonderfully clear and melodious tenor voice and they called him back time after time but all he did was a reprise of "River Shannon." I tried my best to get him to do other musical numbers but he would never sing anything else.

That summer, Ned said, was to be their last in the United States. When we closed the tent he and Edna got in their car and drove away and we never heard of them again.

Altogether, it was a wonderful summer and one of the reasons was that for the first time since we started our own show, I did not have to worry about getting the tent up and down. Quite by accident during the summer of 1935 I heard that Scotty Greenhagen and his lovely wife, who had been on the Chase-Lister Show a number of years, were working a sword box act in a carnival and were very unhappy. I finally caught up with them at Stronghurst, Illinois, and hired Scotty as my canvas boss. The

Greenhagens were with us the last four or five weeks of the season and when we closed they went to visit relatives somewhere in Illinois. While there, Mrs. Greenhagen contracted a throat infection and died, but Scotty showed up for the 1936 season with his little boy, Junior, and an old-time circus canvasman, Shanty Speer—so called because his job in the circus was handling chandeliers. Scotty and Shanty were to stay with us for thirteen years.

House trailers of the homemade variety were just beginning to come into existence then and we acquired one—the frame purchased from a Wapello welder who abandoned his own project and the body built to my specifications by an unemployed carpenter in West Burlington. The trailer was sixteen feet long; it had a little room in front with two settees that let down into beds, a tiny kitchen midships and at the back, over the wheel house, a little bathroom. In the ceiling there was a fifty-gallon water tank for the bath, the water being heated by an immersion heater dropped into the tub. By the standards of the sixties it was a pretty crude affair but compared to the dingy hotel rooms and side-street rooming houses where we had lived so long it was pure luxury.

And Rome Lee finally got to have a dog—a pretty little white puppy, half Spitz and half Collie, that was given to him by a farmer. The pup grew into a large dog with all the lovable, affectionate qualities of the Collie and the feistiness of the Spitz. Rome called him Laddie and in time he became a great watchdog. Before the show he would let children pet him, pull his ears or do anything else but after the show, when the crowd had left the lot and the lights had been turned out, it practically was worth your life to step into the tent. One night Caroline and I went up town after the show to get a bite to eat. It was raining and I put on an old raincoat that I had not worn in some time. When we came back, Laddie did not recognize me and would not let me near the tent until Caroline spoke to him. The first time we played Quincy, Illinois, which was considerably larger than the other towns we had been playing, Laddie seemed to sense something different—or else his instincts told him of some danger we were unaware of. Louise Klein was in our box office, selling tickets. Every night when she opened the box office, Laddie parked himself in front of the door. When she finished, he escorted her all the way around to the back of the tent, staying right with her until she turned the jackbox over to me.

Laddie became as much a part of The Schaffner Players as the players themselves. Every year we got a large number of Christmas cards addressed to Neil, Caroline, Rome Lee and Laddie Schaffner.

5

The effect of our new radio personality was so startling on our tent show patronage that Caroline and I began trying to figure out some way to get better exposure. Our first effort was at WHO. Irving Grossman got us an audition with the program director, but he would have nothing to do with us.

"It's just too corny for words," he said.

"The day will come," I told him, "when WHO will carry this show on network."

After making a sizeable payment on our debts, Caroline and I had a thousand dollars in cash. We decided to take half of it and go into Chicago for a try at big-time radio—promising ourselves that if we had not connected by the time the five hundred dollars was gone we would go back to Carthage, pick up the radio show on WCAZ and do personal appearances again. We told Irving Grossman about this and he said he would give us as big a lift as he could with William Ellsworth, an agent in Chicago who was a friend of his.

We put Rome Lee back in the military academy at Aledo and took off for Chicago with the trailer, which we parked in a cluttered lot behind the Raleigh, an old theatrical hotel on the near north side where I had stayed when trouping in burlesque and vaudeville. We called on Bill Ellsworth, who told us he had received a very glowing report from Grossman, and after I had described our WCAZ program and the following it had, he agreed to become our exclusive agent for the customary fifteen percent commission. That afternoon I paid a call on the Dramatic Publishing Company, which had bought one or two plays from me, and the president, a Mr. Sergel, expressed some interest in *Jittering Spooks* as a likely vehicle for high schools. I dropped the script off the following morning and that afternoon he called me at the Raleigh to ask if I would take two hundred and fifty dollars for the amateur rights. As soon as I caught my breath I said yes and the next morning went down and picked up the check.

On our third day in Chicago, Ellsworth arranged an audition for us at the Wade Advertising Agency, which represented among others the manufacturers of Alka-Seltzer, the sponsor of the Saturday night "National Barn Dance" on the NBC network. Walter Wade, the head of the agency, and two of his assistants, Bill Jones and Pete Lund, sat behind a big desk as Caroline and I stood in the middle of the room, reading from notes on scraps of paper, and went through a typical episode of "Toby's Bugtussle News." None of them showed much interest as we went along and Wade even answered the telephone a couple of times, so when we finished the episode I turned for my coat.

"Let's hear the next episode," said Wade.

We gave them another and got precisely the same reaction as the first time. When I picked up my coat no one asked us to stay but as we left, Ellsworth told us to drop by his office later, and when we did he asked if we would take two hundred dollars for a thirty-day option.

"What's that again?" I asked. "I'm a little hard of hearing."

"Two hundred for a thirty-day option."

"I should say we will!" I said.

In a few minutes, Mrs. Ellsworth appeared with a check for $170—the option less Bill's commission. We had been in town only three days and already had picked up $420. I turned to Caroline and asked, "Where have we been with money like this around?"

Evenings were getting chilly in Chicago and since our only heat in the trailer came from an oil heater that sweated the walls, and since every time we plugged in the immersion heater for a bath we blew a fuse, we found another place to store the trailer and took a nice little apartment in the Dearborn Plaza on North Dearborn Street. Several days passed without further word from the Wade agency. Then Mr. Wade himself called and asked us to come in for a conference. When we got to his office he said he was wondering whether we could do a three-minute comedy spot on the Barn Dance show and I said, "Why sure." He handed us two reserved seat tickets to the Eighth Street Theater and told us to see the show that Saturday night and, as if by afterthought, added that we would go on the following week.

We went to the theater as directed and found the show unlike anything else we had ever seen. People kept running around in funny makeup, cutting up while others were trying to sing, and Caroline was appalled.

"We don't want any of this," she said quite firmly.

"But honey," I said, "they pay people for that—and if that's where the money is that's where we're going to be."

I wrote a script for our spot and turned it in to Pete Lund about the middle of the week and he approved it. On Friday we went up to the NBC studios in the Merchandise Mart to rehearse the show. When our time came, I watched the faces of the production men behind the glass but I could detect no more reaction there than during the audition at the Wade agency. After the rehearsal, Bill Jones came up to me and said, "You know, thirty million people will be listening tomorrow night. Will that bother you?"

"Not at all," I said. "The only thing that bothers me is working without audiences. That's what put us here."

Saturday night we went on the combined NBC network of 550 stations along with Joe Kelly, Uncle Ezra (Pat Barrett), The Maple City Four, Lula Belle & Scotty and all that bunch of headliners. In one of our gags Toby described the headline he had put on a story about Mrs. Astorbilt Morgan's flower show. It read, "Mrs. Morgan's Plants Are Beautiful." Susie said, "That's nice," and Toby said, "Yeah, but I left the *l* out of plants." The reaction from the theater audience was electric. Laughter grew and grew and finally burst into applause.

We did two shows that night, one for the East and one for the West, and although the audience was kind to us we did not have the slightest idea what the reaction among radio listeners or the agency might have been. On Monday we went up to Bill Ellsworth's office and he called Pete Lund. We could hear only one side of the conversation but after a while Ellsworth asked, "How much are they getting?" Then after listening a while longer he said, "They ought to get more than that—they write their own material and all," and then listened some more. Finally he put his hand over the telephone mouthpiece and turned to me.

"Will a hundred and fifty dollars be all right for three minutes?" he asked.

"Yes sir!" I said, and Ellsworth said they wanted us the next Saturday night. They continued to want us from week to week but never offered us a contract.

We had been on the show only a few weeks when the new Hammond electric organ was introduced to the nation on the show. Alec Templeton, the blind pianist, was to play it but when he started not a sound came from the organ. Bill Jones of the agency rushed up and asked if I could go out and kill three minutes. I grabbed Caroline by the hand and took her down to the

mike. We did a bit we had done many times on the tent show,
a thing about how differently a man treats a woman when he is
courting her and when they have been married awhile. The
audience seemed to like it. By the second show they had the
electric organ working so we did not repeat it, but in our pay
envelope for that night we found an extra hundred and fifty
dollars.

In time, Toby and Susie were given the same sort of buildup
that the other stars received and they even let me kid the commercials—something of a radical departure for those days. In a
typical Toby commercial, I read the pitch in the usual serious
manner until I got to that part describing Alka-Seltzer's ingre-
dients. Then I stumbled all over sodium acetyl salicylate.

> TOBY: Sodium setelpate . . . uh, sizzlepate . . . uh, sizzletate
> . . . uh, sizzlerlate . . . sizzling tater.
> JOE KELLY: You're getting hysterical. Do you take Alka-
> Seltzer?
> TOBY: I certainly do. I follow the directions.
> KELLY: What do you mean?
> TOBY: I keep the bottle tightly closed.

We lived very well during those months. Although we sometimes spent more than we had coming in, at Christmas time our
nest egg was bigger than when we came to town. We bought a
lot of presents, brought Rome Lee up from the military academy
and had a wonderful Christmas in the apartment. Each Saturday
night through the winter we appeared on the Barn Dance, building up the names of Toby and Susie. As the first of May approached we began to have some doubts about going back to
the tent show. Many of our show business friends told us we
simply would be crazy to leave when we were so well established as radio comedians and the Wade agency offered all kinds
of blandishments, including public appearances on the fair circuit, to keep us on. Even so, a thousand things pulled us toward
the tent. The show was our own little business. There we were

our own bosses and not at the mercy of anyone except the general public, and we were very sentimental about that. As we reflected on it, we realized that the sight and sound of people—real live people—sitting out front and reacting to what we said and did on the stage was something we cherished very much. Moreover, it was obvious that if "Toby's Bugtussle News" could give such a lift to our business all the publicity we had received from the Barn Dance would add even more to the box office. After a great deal of thought and discussion, we decided we would check out for the time being and go back on the road. We anticipated no difficulty getting back on radio in the fall.

When I told Walter Wade about our decision, he insisted that we return to Chicago every fourth Saturday to do our spot on the Barn Dance as a means of keeping "Toby & Susie" alive for the fall. We agreed to that and while we were talking I mentioned the handbills, window cards and billboards we used to advertise the show and suggested that we bill ourselves as "Direct from the Alka-Seltzer Barn Dance," using the sponsor's slogan, "Alkalize with Alka-Seltzer," across the bottom of all our paper. Wade agreed to that and I asked if Alka-Seltzer would pay for the printing. He asked how much it would cost and after some hurried mental calculation I said five hundred dollars ought to do it.

"Tell the cashier to give you a check on your way out," he said.

The printing bill actually ran to about a thousand dollars but the "Direct from the Barn Dance" advertising did everything we expected it to do. Our business trebled that of 1936. Where they always had loved us they loved us twice as much and everywhere we picked up new fans because of our radio personalities. We also picked up a covey of imitators.

Many repertoire plays, including my own, had a comic character named Susie but until Caroline and I went on radio as "Toby & Susie" no repertoire team that I ever heard of had used the names in that manner to identify themselves. As word of our success got around, "Toby & Susie" teams popped up all over the country and some of the hardly-able little imitator outfits began playing around the edges in our territory, going into towns near those we played and attracting people who expected to see us. They continued to be a nuisance for years.

As long as we were touring the upper end of our territory, going into Chicago every fourth Saturday night for our radio spot was no particular burden, but when we headed down into Missouri I wrote Mr. Wade and asked to be released from our commitment. To my surprise, he agreed readily, saying they would keep "Toby & Susie" alive by having Joe Kelly read a letter from his country cousins every week. Our original plan was to head back north out of Missouri and close the season at Mount Sterling, Illinois, but a committee from the little town of Queen City, Missouri, called on us and asked us to extend our season in order to play their town during a fall festival the third week of September. I thought the town was too small, and the jump too long to make the week profitable but they insisted so strongly that I finally told them we would come for nine hundred dollars flat—and they could keep anything that we took in over that. They took me up, and that meant I had to find a new date for the intervening week between Mount Sterling and Queen City. I looked on the map and picked Kahoka, Missouri, which was about halfway between the two towns.

When I got to Kahoka, I found only one vacant lot that was flat and suitable for our tent. It was three or four blocks from the center of town and was bordered by a barbed wire fence. Several cows were grazing in it. I inquired around and found that it belonged to a Mr. John Gutting, who turned out to be a man in his late seventies. Since Skeeter Kell (who had died a year or so before) had played Kahoka for a number of years with his fine show, I started my pitch by telling Mr. Gutting I had a show like Skeeter's.

"Don't say it's as good as Skeeter Kell's," he said.

"I didn't say it was as good as Skeeter's," I said, "I just said it was like his."

"Wal, I don't know," he said.

He kept walking around as if trying to shake me and I kept following him, urging him to let me have the lot but about all he would say was, "I don't know." Finally, he said he had let the "soldier boys," meaning the American Legion, have a carnival down there and they took all his wire down and did not put it back "and didn't even give me any steeples," meaning staples, to repair it.

"I'm sorry about that, Mr. Gutting," I said, "but I have a legitimate company, a traveling stock company. It isn't anything like a carnival and I'll be glad to see that the wire is put back and I'll pay you fifty dollars. I'll be glad to pay you right now, in advance."

"Wal, I don't know."

After innumerable repetitions of this dialogue, I left Mr. Gutting and drove all over town again trying to find another lot. There just was not one so I returned to the business district. I saw Mr. Gutting coming out of a store and braced him again.

"Got a show like Skeeter Kell's, eh?" he said.

"Yes, sir," I said. "We put on plays and vaudeville."

He kept saying that I had said our show was as good as Skeeter's and I kept saying no, I only said it was like Skeeter's— it was that type of show—and after keeping me dangling for a half hour or so he said he would let me have the lot and took my fifty dollars.

Monday night in Kahoka was cold and drizzly. Around six thirty Mr. Gutting banged on the trailer door.

"There's people over there in front of the tent," he said.

"Well, I don't think they will go away," I said.

Mr. Gutting grinned and said, "You've done this before, ain't you?"

That was the beginning of a great friendship. We played on the Gutting lot for many years and each year we had long visits with him. Before he died he told his son that "Toby is to have that lot as long as he wants it" and the son honored the old man's wish.

We did a good week's business in Kahoka and on Sunday jumped to Queen City in several trucks supplied by the official committee. On arrival we were amazed to find that other merchants did not share the committee's admiration of the show. Thirty of them had signed up for thirty dollars apiece to underwrite our guarantee and by the time we got there some of the pessimists around town had convinced most of them they had made a bad deal. We proceeded to confound them by grossing $1240. In accordance with our deal, I turned $340 over to the committee and at once found myself in a hornet's nest. One faction among the guarantors wanted to put the money in the town treasury and use it to improve the park; another wanted to prorate it among those who signed the guarantee—and both got sore at me because I would not take sides.

Too late, I remembered some fine advice an old Chautauqua booker had given me some years earlier. He said, "Don't ever let 'em make any money. It causes trouble every time. Break even, or make 'em dig up a dollar or two, but don't ever make money!"

6

We had a net profit for the season of five thousand dollars and when we got back into Chicago we rented a somewhat finer apartment than we had had the previous winter. Then we learned that we did not have the Barn Dance deal again. Walter Wade had thought up a slick new radio show called "Stars Over Hollywood," which was to feature a different comedian each week. He signed up a dozen or so New York comedians and to build them up for the new show decided to put one of them on the Barn Dance each week in our spot. The agency nevertheless assured us week after week that we would be going back.

For a while we did not suffer at all in the pocketbook. Bill Ellsworth landed work for me on a recorded radio show starring Billy B. Vann, an old-time musical comedy star. I was paid thirty-five dollars a record—about three times the usual rate for "readers," as they were called—and on some days we cut as many as ten records. When this work ended an old friend, Ken Christy, who was an established radio actor, set me up to audition for a commercial movie being produced for the International Harvester Company by the Chicago Film Laboratory. I landed a character part. When we finished that job I got the leading part in another movie which the laboratory produced for John Morrell & Company, and also landed a small part in it for Tom Gordon, a dear friend who had been in tab shows and vaudeville but who at the time badly needed work. Then a more elaborate movie job came along and I was looking forward to it but they gave my part to Tom. He ultimately became a director for the studio.

Weeks went by without work and it seemed that our money was just melting away. We brought Rome Lee to Chicago for Christmas and had a good time together but after he had returned to school we decided that we had our fill of Chicago. Right after New Year's 1938 we went over to Cedar Rapids, where we had some friends working on Station WMT, and made a deal to go on there with "Toby's Bugtussle News." While I worked on scripts for the show at the hotel, Caroline started out to find an apartment. The very first lady she called said she had rented her apartment but suggested that Caroline leave her name so she could call us if she heard of anything.

"I'm Mrs. Neil Schaffner and we are at the Montrose Hotel," said Caroline.

"Not Neil Schaffner from Fort Dodge?" the lady asked.

"The same," said Caroline.

"Heavens! I used to live right across the street from Neil. I'm Vera Flaherty, formerly Vera Carter. Why don't you come on out and stay with us until you find something?"

We stayed with the Flahertys for a week while we looked for an apartment. Their daughter, Louise, was a senior in high school and was rehearsing for a class play, so she naturally asked if I would help her with her part. She brought her play book home and handed it to me with the remark that "I don't suppose you are familiar with this."

"I should say I am," I said. "I wrote it."

It was *The Ghost Bird*, the title under which the Dennison Play Company had issued *The Vulture* for amateur production. I was a little surprised to find it still being played, although the Dennison Company had told me that in 1929, when they first released it, *The Ghost Bird* was staged by more schools and colleges than any other play except George M. Cohan's *Seven Keys to Baldpate*. We attended the play and enjoyed it very much; Louise turned in a good performance, and the principal introduced us to the audience.

We started in on WMT and arranged amateur contests in Muscatine and several other towns, offering a ten-dollar cash prize for the best performance and a fifty-dollar grand prize at the end of a ten-week elimination. Between the amateur acts, Caroline and I did comedy skits. Meanwhile a salesman on WMT arranged for us to audition at Station WOW in Omaha for the Peterson Baking Company, bakers of Peter Pan bread, and they had offered us a contract starting at about seventy-five dollars a week with options running practically forever. They took "Toby's Bugtussle News" just as it was, with one exception —they wanted a new name. If there was one word that was anathema to bakers it was *bug*, so we called the program "Toby's Corntussle News." Peter Pan put us on a regional network of six stations and we caught on almost at once. In a matter of a few weeks an independent survey showed that we had more listeners in Iowa, Nebraska, western Illinois and northern Missouri than any other show on daytime radio. We started printing an actual *Corntussle News*, offering it free to listeners who wrote in for it. Our first printing was ten thousand copies but we received thirty thousand requests. William Quarton, the station manager, told us in 1965 that "Toby & Susie" still held the WMT record for mail response.

About midwinter Pete Lund called from Chicago to tell us that they were ready for us to come back on the "National Barn Dance." He offered three hundred dollars a week but of course we were tied up by Peter Pan by then and were not very much interested anyway. Our amateur contests were pulling big crowds and we already were making plans for the 1938 tent show season.

We had assumed that we could drop "Toby's Corntussle News" for the summer and pick up again in the fall but the Peterson people had other ideas. They said that dropping the show for the summer was to them the same as putting billboards up for the slack season and taking them down for the busy season. They did not object, however, when we proposed playing a summer stock engagement under the tent at Marion, a suburb of Cedar Rapids, while continuing the Corntussle News. We set up the tent in a lovely park in Marion but for some reason the show did not click, and I again found myself working like a dog. Caroline and I talked it over and decided that whatever else happened we were not going to give up the show. I got in touch with the Peterson people again and, to my surprise, they offered no objection to our going on the road. We went under rep in our old territory—billing ourselves as "Former Stars of the National Barn Dance"—and did almost as much business as we had done in 1937. When we went back on the radio in September the Corntussle show clicked just as it had the winter before. Shortly after we returned to the air George Weber, who had sold a number of syndicated radio programs for the ZIV organization, came to us with a proposition to transcribe the program and sell it to bakers around the country. He and I and Doug Grant, who had become program director of WMT, formed a partnership to distribute and produce the program. Peterson Baking Company liked the idea very much and not only printed an elaborate brochure about us but took us into Chicago to do a "Toby & Susie" act for the National Bakers' Convention at the Edgewater Beach Hotel. On the strength of that, Weber began signing up sponsors and soon we were heard coast-to-coast, in big cities as well as in small towns. (Among our outlets were WOR in New York, KFY in Los Angeles, KOA in Denver, WTMJ in Milwaukee and WOAI in San Antonio.) We received royalties ranging from five to forty dollars a show, depending on the size of the stations, and except for selling expense and the cost of the transcriptions this was all gravy because we were doing the program anyway for the Peterson midwestern network.

About the time the recorded Corntussle News began to catch on, two things happened that pleased us very much. First, the same fellow at WHO in Des Moines who had thought "Toby & Susie" were "too corny for words" back in 1936 when we needed a boost so badly, called me in Cedar Rapids and asked if I could hurry into Des Moines to audition for the Ford dealers of Iowa. I had the pleasure of telling him we were under long-term contract. Then we went into Chicago to do a guest appearance on the Barn Dance, and, sure enough, at the end of the program the announcer said, "Toby & Susie appeared on this program through the courtesy of the Peter Pan Bakers... This is the National Broadcasting Company."

"You see what I said?" I told Caroline.

For fifteen years we had been shipping our tent show equipment from town to town by rail or by commercial trucks but in 1939 we acquired our own transportation—one big semi-trailer and tractor and two straight trucks, plus a trailer especially built to haul our canvas—and we paid cash for it. In 1940, we introduced a new Thursday night feature attraction—a family play with me as the father, Caroline as the mother and Rome Lee, then sixteen, as the son—and it made a tremendous hit. Each summer was bigger than the last and the recorded radio show also kept growing, ultimately being heard on 172 stations in the United States and sixteen in Canada. Money was pouring in and Caroline and I thought we were on our way to becoming millionaires. We bought a new home in Cedar Rapids.

Then came Pearl Harbor. Bakers started pulling in their horns, and that put the kibosh on the transcribed program, though we kept going on the regional network for Peter Pan until 1943. When Peter Pan canceled, Caroline and I decided that after six years of winter radio and summer tent show we were entitled to a vacation. We went out to Hollywood to visit my brother Rome, who had moved out there from Minneapolis. Before leaving Cedar Rapids I wrote a pilot for an hour-long radio show called "Tent Show of the Air," in which we featured a trimmed-down version of one of my plays. The only thing we could get for the recording was a glass-backed acetate record but we packed it well and shipped it ahead by parcel post. While in Hollywood I met an artist's representative who arranged for an audition at CBS and I went over with my recording. When the engineer opened the package the record was broken into a million little pieces.

"Oh well," I told Caroline, "they probably wouldn't have liked it anyway."

I never got around to trying that again but we did take one more fling in radio. A man came out from the Wade agency in Chicago with a proposition to go on WMT for twenty-six weeks under the sponsorship of Green Mountain cough syrup. We told him that a single-station job like that was hardly worth-while but we would do it if at the end of twenty-six weeks the agency would give us a network shot, coast-to-coast, for one of their larger accounts. The man from Wade said he did not see any reason why the agency would not do that, so we went back on the air with "Toby's Corntussle News." After thirteen weeks the agency decided to conduct a test to measure response to the program. In our continuing story, Toby and Susie had come close to getting married several times, so we tied the knot and offered autographed wedding pictures to listeners who wrote in. The agency and the sponsor agreed that the test would run ten days or until we got five thousand requests, whichever came first. I asked the man from Wade whether five thousand requests in ten days would be considered a good showing for this one station and he said, "Yes indeed." We made one announcement on a Friday—just one announcement—and on the following Monday morning we received ten thousand requests for the photograph. I naturally expected a delegation to come out by plane with a contract for a network show. But no one came. Instead, Wade bought "Lum & Abner"; I heard the price was five thousand a week.

That did it. I told Caroline if that was the way radio was run —if we produced a response like that and then the agency turned around and bought another act—then there was no point to it. We completed the twenty-six-week contract and kissed radio goodbye.

Back in the middle-thirties when we first went into Missouri we ran into a rat's nest of license troubles, having to cough up money not only to the towns but to the counties. We got around that by playing under sponsorship of local organizations, giving them ten percent of our gross in return for lot, license and lights. It was a good deal for both of us. The local organization nearly always got the license and use of the lot for nothing and had to pay only for the light bill out of their share of the receipts. We acquired central locations that we never could have managed for ourselves—often a city park or a school yard—and this naturally helped our patronage. The greatest dividend of the sponsorship policy, however, was the association we built with the leaders of all the communities where we played. They became strong boosters of the show and during World War II we would not have made it without them.

Getting from one place to another with a tent show became a monstrous headache during the war. Gasoline for our trucks came under the jurisdiction of the Office of Defense Transportation, which considered tent shows essential and therefore supplied all the gasoline we really needed. Tires, on the other hand, were rationed by boards that came under the Office of Price Administration, and the OPA did not agree with the ODT. We had fifty-six wheels to keep rubber on and we would not have been able to operate if it had not been that good friends in our old established towns from time to time gave us spares from wrecked vehicles and others that materialized mysteriously from places I did not bother to find out about. Instead of suffering, we actually prospered in the tire department. By the war's end we had a stock of spares that reached to the ceiling of one of our trucks.

Finding actors became harder and harder as Uncle Sam dipped deeper into the manpower barrel and as the demands for war production grew. Finding young men with 4F draft classifications and any talent became practically impossible and many capable older acting people either went into war jobs or turned to more lucrative employment in the nightclubs that mushroomed all over the country. Even though Rome Lee took over a full line of leads in 1942, our standard cast soon became three men and six women—just the opposite of the usual repertoire company. I rewrote dozens of plays to make the characters fit the available people and in 1942 I wrote a new play, *Toby Goes to Washington,* in which Toby was a small-town newspaper editor and all of the characters except the boy and girl were mature people. The play capitalized on all the talk and fear of Nazi spies (this was the period when they caught the saboteurs on the East Coast and still were rounding up others who had worked for Germany under the cloak of various German-American organizations). It was a big hit. Our business kept on building throughout the war. Caroline and I began to enjoy some of the pleasures that other people took for granted. Among other things, we took ballroom dancing lessons and joined a formal dancing club. I bought a new tuxedo. For the first time in our life together we did not worry about a thing.

PART FIVE

Places!

———————

Places!

———————~~~~———————

1

THE TERRITORY WE HAD CARVED OUT FOR THE SCHAFFNER PLAYERS covered about forty thousand miles—the southeastern quarter of Iowa, the northern third of Missouri and a sliver of Illinois along the Mississippi River. After World War II the farms became larger and the farmers fewer; some of the towns lost population, some gained, but overall the region remained essentially as it had been before—rural, friendly and prosperous. Many of our towns were very small and in some we actually could seat every man, woman and child in the tent and have room left. All of them, large and small, were amazingly loyal. On a sultry summer evening in 1948 I was sitting on a park bench in front of the tent in Lewistown, a village of about six hundred in northern Missouri, trying to explain to a visiting journalist from the East how we could have had a packed house the night before. Most of the people, I explained, had come in from farms all around, and although this was their busiest time of the year most of them came every night. In fact, I said, among them were many who had never missed a single performance of our show in Lewistown. The journalist was plainly skeptical but I no sooner had made the statement than our conversation was interrupted by a man whose wind-burned face and rough hands revealed his vocation.

"Toby, I want you to settle an argument," he said. "How long have you been coming here?"

"This is our fourteenth year," I said.

"First time was in the old opera house that used to be over there on the corner, wasn't it?"

"That's right."

"Well, that's what I told Mamma. We haven't missed a single night of your show in all these years."

We did our best to reciprocate for this kind of loyalty. During the war we got our prices back up to the 1929 level—fifty cents for adults and twenty-five for children on the front door, plus a quarter for the reserved chairs—and although the prices of everything else advanced after the war we held the line. We also retained the blues so that people who did not want to spend money for the reserved chairs or who could not afford it could see the show for the price of general admission. We continued to play under local auspices; we sold our advertising banners and offered our prize candy. And the show had the same format as always—a half-hour orchestra concert, a full three-act play and vaudeville between the acts.

The show proper began when the orchestra swung into "Corntussle Capers," the theme of our old radio show, and I popped out on the orchestra platform for my nightly warm-up. I had been doing this for years before I heard the term used in radio, but it had the same purpose—to get them laughing before the payoff jokes started coming—and also to tell them about the play they were about to see and who was going to play what. (We never had printed programs.) It went something like this:

> We've got the best derned show you've seen today. Our play tonight is called Her Unexpected Husband. There's only one reason we call it that—that's the name of it. This play is in three acts and each act comes right after the one before it. There are two scenes in the first act. By that I mean the curtain will go down in the middle of the act,

then go right back up again and when it goes up it is later
than it was when it went down. Actually, the second scene
is three days later. We could jist let you set there for three
days, but we'll put 'er all on tonight. Now here's the characters you will meet in this play: First you'll meet John
Watts. That part will be played by Roy Hillard and he's
a derned good actor. Next feller is a Marine by the name
of Bill Watts and that part will be played by our leading
man, Wayne Wellman...and, girls, he is *single*...You
will recognize Wayne any time you see him around town.
He drives a canary yellow Chrysler convertible—or whatever the girl happens to have...Then we've got a couple
of gals in the play...the Boone Sisters...Corinne Boone
will be played by Marsha Powell and Barbara—she doesn't
like to be called Bab because her last name is Boone—will
be played by Hildegarde Saunders. Now I've told all my
actors what a swell bunch of folks you are here in Mt.
Pleasant, so whatever you do, don't let me down. When
each one makes his first appearance give him a swell hand
...You know, give him a good old Mt. Pleasant welcome,
then set back and he'll work his fool head off to please you
...Of course when *I* come on, you know what to do then
... 'cause I'll be playing——

All the kids down front—being well trained over the years—
would yell in unison, "Toby!" Then I would go on:

Of course I didn't forgit the mainmost one in the play.
There is the mamma of the family and that part is played
by——

And all the kids would yell, "Susie!"

I gave this same speech, or a version of it suited to the particular play, every night during the week and if I had not done so
people would have thought part of the show had been left out.
Often I would pretend to be miffed at the attention Susie was
getting from the audience.

"She's hard enough to live with without you giving her more
applause than you gave me," I would say. "If you don't watch
out she'll start thinking she's as good as I am."

Then I would say, "All those that think I'm the best, let me hear you!" They would give me a big round of applause and I would leave the stage. Then Susie would come out and she would get a much bigger ovation. I would come back out and say, "Just for that, I ain't gonna be in it," and stalk down off the stage and out in the audience. I would find an empty seat and sit down.

"Go ahead and have it without me."

Susie would come to the footlights and say, "Oh, Toby, come on—it won't be any good without you!"

"You'd say that whether you thought it or not," I would say, and Susie would reply, "You'd think it whether I said it or not."

Susie would coax some more and at last I would say, "Well, maybe I'll be in it." Then I would stand up and address the audience: "Should I?" They would applaud like mad and I would go back up on the stage and start the show.

I started trying to make Toby as much a part of the audience as of the play away back on the Clyde Gordonier show. In asides to the audience, talking behind my hand, I often gave them my own interpretation of what the villain really was up to, or let them in on what was going to happen next. When we got our own show one of my favorite stunts was to let the audience know when an actor blew his lines.

"That ain't the way it's supposed to be," I would say, "He was supposed to say . . ." and then repeat the line the way it was written. This often blew the actor sky high and I would go into the wings and come back with the script and hand it to him.

"They paid full admission and are entitled to the full thing," I would say, "so read it."

One night when two people went higher than kites during the opening scene, I walked out from the wings and said, "Maybe we oughta practice 'em before we put 'em on." We lowered the curtain, let it stay down a minute or two, then started all over again.

Most of these antics sprang from spur of the moment inspiration. Once when Rome Lee blew his lines I started bawling him out.

"If I had loused up a scene like that with my father," I said, "he would have slapped me up to a peak and slapped the peak off."

"Fine father you must have had!" Rome shot back.

"Damned sight better than you've got!" I said.

The plot of our play *Hillbilly Hoedown* revolved around the plan of a railroad to build through a mountain area against the wishes of the people. In one town our show lot was near the railroad and just when the old man in the play said, "They hain't gonna bring no engine trains up here—how they gonna git 'em up them mountains?" a train whistled.

"Well, they're doin' it," I said.

The panels in our scenery were held by turnbuckles and in making the set one day someone failed to turn them securely. At a tense moment in the play an actor slammed a door and a panel fell out of the wall.

"That's the trouble with them prefabs," I said.

One night I was doing a scene with a cute little ingenue and on sudden inspiration I turned to the audience and said: "I don't understand why them other fellers git to make love to pretty gals and I never do, when I'm better lookin'." Then I turned to the ingenue and said, "Boy, I'm a lover too! Want me to show you?" She began to pull back and I turned once more to the audience, "Shall I kiss her?" The kids all yelled, "Yes!" Caroline was in the wings and decided to get in on the fun. While I had my back to her she stuck her head out and nodded knowingly to the audience, then withdrew. The laughter gave me a clue to what was going on, so I went to a window and pretended to look for Susie. While I was doing this, Susie slipped in and took the ingenue's place. I slipped my arm around her and turned around, all puckered up. When I saw it was Susie instead of the

ingenue, I dropped my arm and said, "Guess we'd better go back
to the play."

Our audiences became so conditioned to this kind of nonsense
that it was not difficult at all to bring them into the play itself
when that was desirable. In *The Girl Next Door*, the audience
actually supplied a key line leading up to the final curtain. One
character was an old man who was a chronic liar. All through
the play, when anyone mentioned having done anything at all
he claimed to have done it "back in nineteen seventeen." In the
final scene, Toby and Susie were on the stage alone.

> SUSIE: Toby, won't you come in and have some nice
> warm breakfast?
> TOBY: I haven't had a warm breakfast since——

The audience came right in: "Nineteen seventeen!"

> TOBY: No, it was long before that.
> (Curtain)

Actually, our show never stopped. Even the talk I gave after
the second act for the purpose of advertising the next night's
bill was designed to get laughs. In 1951 I rewrote *Chain Stores*
and called it *What Mothers Don't Know*. I talked it up this way:

> Now folks, on Thursday night we're gonna bring you
> our feature play of the week ... a brand new comedy that
> will keep you laughin' from the time it starts 'till it's all
> over ... We call it *What Mothers Don't Know*. You know,
> lots of times you hear a mother say, "I tell you, I keep my
> eyes on *my* daughter." Oh yeah! ... Well, in this play the
> mamma has two daughters ... and she keeps one eye on
> one and the other eye on the other, but what goes on
> between them eyes is a caution! ... And girls, you know
> a lot of times your mamma will say to you, "When I was
> a girl, I never *thought* of doing the things you girls do."
> Maybe that's why she didn't do 'em ... Anyhow, if you
> want a bundle of laughs and if you want to see a derned
> good story, don't miss WHAT MOTHERS DON'T
> KNOW, Thursday night.

Only once during the week did I become serious. On closing night before the last act of the play, I stepped out on the orchestra platform, took off my Toby wig and said something like this:

> Friends, this is the last time I'll get to talk to you this year. For many years it has been my pleasure to stand on this platform and welcome you into my tent on opening night. Then when the end of the week comes it is my sad duty to say farewell. I am deeply grateful to you, my friends, because it has been your loyalty and the loyalty of thousands like you that has made this organization possible. The Schaffner Players is more than a show. It is a tradition. It is the life work of Mrs. Schaffner and myself. We have dedicated our lives to it. If we have been able to bring a little fun and laughter into the lives of people we feel that we have not lived in vain. After the next act of this play, the big tent will be torn down and loaded on our fleet of trucks and taken away over to Burlington, where we will be all next week. If any of you happen to be over there and have missed any of the plays this week, we hope you will pay us a visit. A feeling of sadness always comes over us at the end of our engagement here because we realize that another milestone in this thing called life will have passed before we meet again, but we *will meet again!* We will be back next year with new plays, new music, in fact everything new except the name. And now, friends, until we have the pleasure of meeting again at this same time next year, the best of luck to all of you. I thank you.

One of the reasons people came back year after year, I suppose, was that they knew what to expect, in the same way that they knew what to expect of a favorite long run television show on which they had come to know the characters. But another reason was that they got a lot for their money. When Broadway had gone almost exclusively to the one-set play, we often offered two or three sets. This became possible through a basic set of scenery which I designed and which was built by Jesse Cox of Estherville, Iowa, who much earlier had revolutionized road-show scenery with his invention of a method for painting with diamond dyes. The set consisted of flats of many different types and widths, a variety of window pieces and a "Dutchman" for making arches. Each flat contained a removable panel occupying about sixty percent of its surface and we built a large number of panels, covered with various wallpapers, so that different room decorations could be provided easily. Later Jay Bee Flesner, who was practically our right hand for several years, developed a wagon stage for us—two platforms on rails. One set could be erected on a spare platform while another was on stage. We did a show called *The Devil and a Woman* for which Jay Bee built eleven different impressionistic settings such as those usually seen only in the so-called experimental theater. (Jay Bee also turned in a powerful performance as the Devil.) For another play, *Mary's Ankle*, we developed a moving back curtain with a view of a city so that the opening scene could take place on shipboard, giving the illusion of a ship moving away from its dock. When unusual props were required by the story or helped to get laughs, we got them. For my play *Uncle Sol and His Hadacol*, I wrote a scene in which Uncle Jim, who is always borrowing things, persuades Uncle Sol to let him use his typewriter, solemnly pledging to return it in A-1 condition. He returns it and when Uncle Sol sits down to write the typewriter flies apart, pieces scattering all over the set. I had the trick typewriter built especially for the scene. In one of the numerous versions of *Clouds and Sunshine* which we did over the years Caroline and I developed a scene in which Susie is carrying on a gossipy conversation with another character while Toby is putting fertilizer and water on plants around the room. Susie is wearing a hat covered with flowers and each time he passes her, Toby tosses a little fertilizer and a little water on her hat. Soon the flowers begin to grow. We did this by putting the flowers on little springs, which were compressed by means of a thread that Caroline held in one hand. As she released the tension on the thread, the springs relaxed and the flowers appeared to grow.

Another effect involved a scene in which Toby goes to a moon-shiner to get a jug of whiskey, carrying his own jug. The moon-shiner fills the jug and Toby tells him to charge it; the moonshiner refuses to do this so Toby tells him to pour the liquor back where he got it and return the jug. As the moon-shiner exits again, Toby breaks the jug. A big sponge falls out and he picks it up, squeezes out a tin cup full of liquor and drinks it as the curtain falls.

2

After the war it became increasingly difficult to recruit the kind of acting people we needed. Most of the experienced reper-toire actors who had drifted into other lines never came back because there was not enough work for them. All but a handful of the standard repertoire shows had disappeared and those that remained worked only during the summer. Winter house rep had become a thing of the past. A few hardy old-timers did stay around, working club or school dates in the off season, but often we had to take chances on people we never had heard of before. Once we hired a man and his wife as leading team on the under-standing that they were thoroughly experienced. When they got to Wapello for rehearsals we soon discovered the man was rela-tively inexperienced and that his wife had never worked any-thing but a chorus line. She was very attractive, though, and with her show business background I thought she might make it, but she was completely over her depth. At the end of the first week of rehearsal she and her husband slipped out, bag and bag-gage, not even leaving their parts. Another time we hired a hand-some young man who claimed to have worked in a number of dramatic productions but who plainly could not cut it with us. He fortunately saved us the bother of firing him; at the end of the first week he came over to the trailer and handed his parts to Caroline.

"I have decided that I cannot sacrifice my career," he said, "by appearing with so many amateurs."

Of necessity, we turned more and more to youngsters who had no professional experience. Many of them came out of dramatic schools. As far back as I can remember, repertoire actors always had looked down on dramatic school actors—the very term, to their way of thinking, being the lowest that could be applied to anyone in show business. Lower even than carnival people. (You see, show people were very status conscious. Stock company actors felt superior to repertoire; musical tab and repertoire actors looked down on each other and both felt superior to carnival people, who felt superior to medicine show people.) I encountered my first drama school graduate when I was working house repertoire, long before my tent show days. In one play he had to walk up left, turn back and say, "My son, a thief!" As he went through this business at rehearsal, I thought I saw his lips moving and concluded that he was counting his steps. He took ten steps between each position. Sure enough, when we got into a small opera house he walked clear off the stage before speaking his line. Later, after we had our own tent show, I hired a young actor named Ramon Rodriguez. He spent much time in the dressing room poring over Stanislavsky and other books on the theory of acting and when in the wings awaiting his cue he walked up and down trying to get himself in a proper mood for his entrance. More often than not he became so absorbed with mood that he missed his cue and I had to push him on.

After the war, however, many of the better universities and organizations like the Pasadena Playhouse and the Goodman Theater, an adjunct of the Art Institute of Chicago, began doing a much better job of getting across to youngsters what the theater was all about and we got many fine young people from them. One who came from the Goodman was a beautiful, hard-working girl named Delores Heft. She became very popular with our audiences. Morie Grossman, an old rep actor who then was in business in Hollywood, came on the show for a visit and was so impressed by Delores that he got her a screen test, a starlet contract and eventually an audition with Randolph Scott. Delores wrote us that she read her part "just the way I had done on The Schaffner Players" and that Scott immediately said, "That's the one I want." As Delores Dorn she was Scott's leading lady in *Bounty Hunters* and landed lead roles in a number of other movies. She was married for a time to Franchot Tone.

We never really could tell whether these youngsters had it until they appeared before our audiences. Often we were completely fooled. I always had believed that the main ingredient in an actor's ability to establish rapport with his audience was a fervent desire to please. Those who did not get across, it seemed to me, felt they were doing an audience a favor. This, I found, was not always the case. One young man who came on our show seemed to have all the attributes: he was good looking, had a nice speaking voice and spoke his lines convincingly. I never saw a boy who so much wanted to make good as an actor, yet there was something about him that did not go over. Watching him from out front, as I often did, I shared the audience's reaction. When he made an entrance it always seemed to me that someone had just left.

Rome Lee, who had developed into a polished leading man, continued to add strength to our cast until 1949, his last year in medical school (he now is an ophthalmologist in Cedar Rapids), when he had to leave the show. After that Caroline and I found ourselves involved as full-time teachers. We had to teach posture, diction, voice control, how to memorize rapidly and accurately —all the fundamentals of acting—and our tutoring continued throughout the season. And distasteful as it often became, we also had to be full-time chaperones. Since we played in so many very small towns, The Schaffner Players literally lived in a goldfish bowl. People simply adored our young people so long as they were neat and exemplary in behavior, but let them appear on the streets dirty and unkempt or let them violate the accepted rules of personal behavior and the wrath of the whole community came down on them. Gossip spreads quickly in a small town and we warned all the youngsters about this when they came on the show. We laid down strict rules: no liquor around the tent (we never had permitted this); no dating of town boys by the girls; no public lovemaking among themselves; cleanliness and neat appearance. All who signed on with us knew that violation of the rules was cause for notice. I am proud to say that the bad apples among them were few; most were clean-cut kids—well behaved, earnest, hard working and eager to learn. They gave the show a kind of freshness that probably played an important part in our continuing success. Our biggest problem was not keeping them out of trouble but protecting them from the erosive effects of public adulation. On the last day of rehearsal each year I made the same little speech:

"Don't let these towners throw you. They will shower you with attention and many of them will tell you, 'You are the best Toby and Susie ever had.' They will be sincere enough about it, but just take it from me that they've said the same thing to every ingenue and leading man we ever had. The only time you need to worry is when they don't tell you that you are the best."

While we offered a tremendous amount of entertainment for the money, Caroline and I never let ourselves forget that the thing people really came to see was the play. The whole show gravitated around the play and one of the reasons The Schaffner Players kept going when other tent repertoire shows fell by the wayside is that we kept giving the public lively, entertaining and topical plays. We never went all out for comedy; on every repertoire we had at least one gripping drama and in all of our plays we tried to develop a strong story line.

Titles always had played an extremely important role in repertoire, where each night's attendance depended in large part on how successful the manager was in talking up the play to the previous night's audience. Many of our plays had provocative titles: *Right Bed, Wrong Husband, The Stork Laid an Egg, Natalie Needs a Nightie, Inlaws and Outlaws, Meddling Mothers* and *Behind the Country School House,* to mention a few. Often we tried out half a dozen titles before we found one that worked. One of our plays was a farce that I thought was as good as any I had ever written but it did not pull them in until we came up with *His Brother's Honeymoon.* Back in the thirties we revived the old-time book play, *Rebecca of Sunnybrook Farm,* but under that title it laid an egg. As *Her Unwelcome Relative* it caught on. In the early fifties, when a new generation of show-goers had come along, we polished it up again and it did very well under the original title.

There was nothing particularly original about this title switching. Many years ago a play called *Up in the Haymow* closed in New York almost before it opened. The title was changed to *Getting Gertie's Garter* and it was an instant success.

Caroline and I tried even harder after World War II to develop plays on topical themes. When the boys came home, we wrote a warm little love story called *The Girl Next Door;* when William Boyd was going strong as Hopalong Cassidy, we wrote a western farce called *Hopalong Toby* and when Art Linkletter was garnering huge television audiences with "People Are Funny" we did one called *How Funny Are People.* (Both were satires on the programs.) In 1948, when there was a spate of newspaper exposés about marijuana parties in Hollywood and about the drug traffic generally, we rewrote my prohibition play, *Why Girls Walk Home,* and called it *Once in a Blue Moon.* The story revolves around the efforts of a gangster to compromise the town's crusader by putting his identical twin in situations that embarrass him. In the prohibition version, the twin was spirited out of an insane asylum; in *Blue Moon*, he is a shell-shocked victim from a nearby veterans' hospital. In the earlier version the twin kept trying to find his lost sweetheart, Marianne; in the second he talks throughout the play to his imaginary pet kangaroo. At the time, I insisted that it was mere coincidence that Brock Pemberton's very funny play, *Harvey*, still was going strong on the road and in the movies. Actually, we wrote *Once in a Blue Moon* only after we had tried unsuccessfully to lease *Harvey*.

Toby's enduring favor with audiences was due in large part, I think, to the fact that he continued to evolve throughout the years even while giving the impression of never changing. It would have been silly for me to portray him as the young farm boy when I looked more like the farmer and so as I grew older Toby grew older in the plays. Yet the red wig, the freckles and the peaked eyebrows remained and the basis of much of his humor held constant. Toby assumed, for example, that the city slicker was the unlettered one, not he, and he never overlooked an opportunity to demonstrate this. To a lady from the city he might say, "I've got to go out and oil the hogs," and she would say, "Oh yes, I heard them squeaking when I came in." Or he would ask, "Want to stay for supper? We're gonna have windmill soup." The visitor would ask, "What in the world is windmill soup?" and Toby would reply, "If it goes around, you git some."

Poking fun at rural customs remained one of Toby's favorite pastimes, yet the subjects of conversation changed with the times. Back in the twenties, when some farmers still drove buggies to town and many more tilled their fields with teams, our plays with farm settings nearly always had an old lady on stage with a churn. Toby would be mending harness and someone forever was sending him to the well to fetch water. After World

War II, when everyone drove cars and tilled their fields with tractors, the little old lady tended her flowers and read the farm magazines and Toby talked knowingly about corn pickers, hybrids and weed killers.

When prepared poultry feeds came into use and the manufacturers were making all sorts of claims for them, Toby talked about feeding his chickens "some of that Lay or Bust." When asked what that was, Toby replied, "That's the name of the chicken feed, Lay or Bust." At that moment an explosion was heard offstage and Toby explained, "The rooster got hold of some of it." In one of my early plays, Toby comes home from a trip to town in a wagon and explains why he is so late: "Couldn't help it. On the way home I picked up the preacher and from then on them mules couldn't understand a word I said." The postwar Toby takes a load of hogs to town in a truck and relates how he drove all the way home at seventy miles an hour. Asked why, he replies, "Truck ain't got no brakes and I wanted to git home before anything happened."

All through the years, much of Toby's humor was built upon his doing exactly what he was told to do—no more, no less. In an early play, his employer directs him to "run over to see how Old Mrs. Brown is today." He comes back and says, "She wouldn't tell me." "She wouldn't tell you what?" the employer asks and Toby replies, "How old she is." Post-Korean War Toby is an aging chauffeur. When his employer gives him the keys to his new Cadillac he carefully instructs Toby on following the operations manual to the letter. Later Toby appears, explaining he is late because he had to get a truck to tow the Cadillac. "Why in the world did you have to do that?" the employer asks and Toby, holding up the manual, says, "It says right here that the car should not be driven more than two thousand miles without changing oil. The speedometer turned two thousand when I was twenty miles out and. . . ."

The Toby in all my plays pretended to be a Lothario but the audience could plainly see that he wasn't. In one of his earliest gags Toby tells about attending a party where they played "bobbing for apples." Any fellow who did not get an apple out of the tub with his teeth had to hold his head under water until some girl promised to kiss him. "I'd have drowned if my sister hadn't been there," Toby says. As he grew older Toby's interest in the girls became much more direct, but someone always still beat his time. In one play Toby complains about this:

> Dad burn that Bud Hawkins! He's tryin' to cut me out
> with Flaxie. Last night when I was over to see her, he
> was there . . . We was all three of us in the parlor . . . settin'
> on the squattee . . . Flaxie was in the middle, I was on this
> end and Bud was on that end. Just then the lights went out.
> Dad burn it was embarrassin'. Whenever I'm with a girl
> and the lights go out I always feel for the poor girl . . . Bud
> Hawkins got the same idea . . . It was embarrassin' 'cause
> neither of us knew that Flaxie had gone to fix the fuse.

Much of Toby's humor always had been visual. Being more easily shocked by what the younger people had to say in his later years, the double take and triple take assumed increasing importance. But one of the most powerful weapons in his arsenal was what I always have called the no-take. In one scene Toby is seated, in earnest conversation with another character. A rifle shot is heard offstage and Toby's hat goes flying through the air. Instead of jumping up in fright or hiding under the table, as he might be expected to do, he does not move. He stares blankly ahead. Then, slowly, a hand reaches down and carefully feels an ankle, then a shin, a knee, a thigh, the stomach and chest and finally the head. Then he heaves a huge sigh of relief and a silly smile spreads slowly across his face. That kind of response never failed to bring down the house.

In time Toby became not the boy next door but the man next

door, or down the street. In one play he was the aging farm hand, in another the hog buyer, the country editor, the truck driver or the private detective—a shrewd, fast-talking reminder of someone everybody in the audience knew. Everything was fair game for him, especially television. When a cigarette company had a big advertising campaign going about "what's up front" of the filter, he watched a woman character, generously endowed in the derriere, as she flounced up the stairs. Then he turned to the audience and asked, "Are you sure it's what's up front that counts?" When *Wagon Train* was a big night attraction, Toby listened while a catty girl in the play bragged about how she was going to win a beauty contest. "She's got as much chance of winning," he tells the audience, "as that wagon train has of getting to California."

Securing plays suitable for our audience became increasingly difficult from the middle-thirties onward. New York plays generally were unsuited for our family audiences and royalties on the few plays that we might have used were far beyond our reach. While a large number of tent repertoire shows were on the road, at least a few acceptable plays were written by other actor-authors but by the end of World War II nearly all of them were gone. Caroline and I were forced to write our own, and it was fortunate for us that after 1945 we never had to troupe in winter. That gave us time to concentrate on our repertoire. With seven new bills to produce each season, we never would have made it if it had not been possible to secure permission from other authors, or their heirs, to rewrite old plays that had been successful in repertoire. We would not have made it, either, if we had not assumed that it was our business only to entertain. We had no interest in trying to revolutionize the theater or to solve the great problems of society; we felt the theater had fulfilled its entire purpose when it entertained, and our plays must have had some merit in that respect. The customers kept coming.

3

In June 1948 Donald Wayne described our show in *Holiday Magazine* as "the nearest thing to a living folk theater that America has." I had never thought of it that way, but we qualified on both of Webster's counts: our plays certainly were "pertaining to the folk" and they "originated ... among the common people." We found a great many of our characters, as a matter of fact, right in the towns where we played, or on our own show.

A popular character in repertoire theater always had been the G-string—an old man, usually portrayed as having a high, squeaky voice that resembled the sound of the G string on the violin. G-string characters abounded all over our territory. The constable in my play *Be Yourself* came straight from a police officer in Iowa City who coined many words and phrases of his own by switching words around in his sentences so that what he said was not what he meant to say. He said such things as "he's too inde-gosh-darned-pendent," "he got himself up in a heaval," and "you can kiss my so-and-so and I'm just the one who can do it." He coined the word *necessitary* and once when trying to flush a group of college boys from behind some bushes, where they had pretended to hide from him, he said: "You come out from behind those bushes or I'll get somebody who will." The sheriff in *Toby Takes the Town* was patterned after Chester Espey, who worked for us a number of times as advance agent. Chester could not make a simple report on how he had squared a town without talking about everything in the wide world before getting to his point.

A lady in Geneseo, Illinois, with whom I roomed early in my career, became the model for a number of our comedy old-maid characters. When this dear lady could trap a listener she sat in her rocking chair, rocking back and forth, talking in a flat monotone in perfect cadence with her rocking. She talked, then gig-gled, then talked some more, but always in cadence. Once I came down the stairs and she started talking as soon as she saw me, as if we were resuming some interrupted conversation. "I've kept all ... kinds of roomers ... but I've always been ... very par-ticular of the kind ... I get ... Well, sir, one night ... I was sit-ting here and ... there came a rap ... at the door and ... there was a man ... and a woman ... standing there ... and I didn't think ... they were mar-ried ... and sure enough ... they asked ... for sep-arate rooms ... Well, sir, I put ... her upstairs ... and him downstairs ... Says I to myself ... I'll keep my eye ... on those people ... Well, sir, sure ... enough, along ... in the night ... I heard a door ... open ... and ... I heard ... some steal-thy steps ... out in the hall ... and I walked out ... in the hall and ... there he was ... trying to get ... in her room ... and I held up ... my lamp ... and said, 'Back! ... There'll ... be no night ... walking here.' "

We advertised The Schaffner Players as "America's Only Living Folk Theater" and this attracted a new, though small clientele among young people who had never come to see us be-fore. In 1949 Vance Johnson wrote an article for *Collier's* which dealt with tent repertoire and Toby generally, but paid con-siderable attention to our show. Among other things, he said that "Toby is as much revered in his territory as John Barrymore ever was on Broadway," and after this article appeared many of the metropolitan newspapers in the Middle West sent their top writers out to look the show over and write feature stories for their Sunday magazines. Most of these people were amazed by the show. We were doing *How Funny Are People* when Francis A. Klein, the drama critic of the St. Louis *Globe-Democrat* paid us a visit. After the final curtain he came back to the dressing room and stood in the door several minutes without saying any-thing. After a while I looked up and said, "Well?"

"My editor isn't going to believe me when I tell him this is
one of the best shows I ever saw, at any time, at any price," he
said.

In his write-up Klein said, "Blasé boy wonders could take
lessons from this veteran tent show trouper. Toby is as midwestern as the tall corn."

All this publicity drew people out from the cities—those who
had never heard of tent repertoire before and those who had not
been to a show since their childhood. Television came along and,
surprisingly, it helped business even more. Perhaps this was because live television, which boomed for a few years before
Hollywood took over the medium, whetted an interest in live
theater in a way that the movies never had. As time went on,
television gave us one of our greatest boosts.

In 1953 I chanced to pick up *The New York Times* and read
an article by Don Carle Gillette about a man named Hannon
who was supposed to have written many Toby plays. The article
annoyed me and I wrote Gillette that I had never seen a play by
this man and did not know of anyone else who had, and this was
the start of a fine friendship. Don wrote an article about us for
the *Times* titled "Toby Thrives in the Tents." In the early summer of 1954 we were playing Mt. Pleasant when a messenger
came over to the tent and said I had a long distance call from
New York. The caller was Paul Feigay, the executive producer
of the TV Workshop of the Ford Foundation. He said he had
read this article in the *Times* and wanted to know if it was really
true that we were putting plays on under a tent and that people
actually paid to see them. I told him it was true.

"The world should know about this," he said.

"Well, I'm perfectly willing for the world to know," I said.
"Come on out any time you can."

I sent Feigay our itinerary and shortly thereafter he wired
me that he would join us on our opening night at Delta, Iowa.
We were playing a hillbilly show I had put together called

Stump Holler Folks and I naturally wanted to put our best foot forward so I noised it around considerably that some distinguished television producers were going to visit our show that night. Delta has a population of about five hundred but at curtain time nearly a thousand people were in the tent. During the first act a horrific rain and windstorm struck. Water just poured down and the wind lifted the tent up and popped it down on the center poles with such force that we had to stop the play. No one could hear what we were saying. One of the actors went out front and led the audience in a community sing while the others pulled slickers over their costumes and went out into the storm to loosen guy ropes, which shrank when they got wet, and to pound stakes pulled by the shrinking ropes. Just as the storm struck one of the boys came around from the front of the tent and informed me the gentlemen from New York had arrived, but I did not have time even to greet them. A storm always made me nervous as a setting hen; if a tent should collapse a lot of people could get hurt and while the rain and wind lasted I moved all around, keeping one eye cocked on the storm and another on the tent. Fortunately, the worst of it passed rather quickly and as soon as we could be heard we resumed *Stump Holler Folks* as though nothing had happened.

Feigay and his associate, Rickey Leacock, stayed with us two or three days, watching our plays and studying the audiences. Each night they circulated among the people waiting for the box office to open, asking them about their habits—whether they had television in their homes, whether they went to the movies, and so on—and about why they came to the show. Nearly all of our patrons had television sets, of course, and most of them occasionally went to the movies. Many read books with some regularity. They found it difficult, though, to explain just why they came to see Toby and Susie. "We just always have," they would say, "because it's the thing to do." Many said they had started coming as children and now brought their own children. Before departing for New York, Feigay said he had decided to make a movie on the show for the Ford Foundation's Sunday night television spectacular, "Omnibus." He and Leacock came back several weeks later, accompanied by Russell Lynes of *Harper's Magazine*, who wrote the script, and a crew of about ten. They made movies while we played to huge crowds at Shelbina and La Plata, Missouri. The show went over with a bang.

Toward the end of the 1954 tent season we thought we were getting another break that we long had hoped for. Dan Goldberg, who had been a partner with Jules Feiffer in the production of a show called *Goodnight Ladies* that had a long run in Chicago and then went on tour, leased *Natalie Needs a Nightie* for a tour as a one-piece attraction. Caroline and I were terribly disappointed by it. The cast did not compare with ours on the tent show; they did not grasp the lightness of the farce or appreciate what a fast-moving play it was. The production was even worse. Instead of a nice set of scenery showing the bachelor's apartment in New York, the way we produced it, Goldberg had an old drape set. The show opened in Oshkosh, Wisconsin, and then played Minneapolis, Kansas City, Cleveland and several other cities for about ten weeks. In each city the critics roasted both the production and the acting, but most of them noted that the audiences laughed heartily and long.

The "Omnibus" show, titled "Toby in the Tall Corn," was televised in November 1954 and Caroline and I were delighted with the manner in which it was done. The show won the Edinburgh Film Festival Award as the best television documentary of 1954 and *Look* ran a big article about the award and carried my picture. "Omnibus" repeated the show in the spring, causing a great deal of additional comment that helped our business during the 1955 season. As a result of the show, the *Saturday*

Evening Post assigned Joe Alex Morris to do an article about us. Ivan Dmitri, the great color photographer, came out to make pictures for the article, intending to stay three days. He fell in love with the show and stayed three weeks, laughing and applauding like a kid who had never been to a show in his life. He did a beautiful job and so did Morris. The article was factual and did us the honor of not looking down the nose at us, but some smart-aleck editor whose job it was to write titles for articles called it "The Corniest Show on the Road." I nearly had apoplexy. If there was a word in the English language that did not fit The Schaffner Players it was that word *corny*. It suited us just fine that the *Post* did not get around to printing the story until September when we were closing for the season.

From 1956 on, newspaper and magazine writers were frequent visitors. Practically all of them had the same series of reactions. First, they were astounded by the size of our crowds. Then they saw the plays; none was at all like the William Inge and Tennessee Williams plays so popular on Broadway, but they could see for themselves that the audiences liked them, so they concluded that people in the Middle West were terribly naïve. Then they took a closer look at the audience and found that it included doctors, lawyers, merchants, farmers and people from all walks of life, among whom were many who attended the theater in Chicago, New York and other places as well. After a night or two, most of them had a first-rate case of frustration—finding themselves wholly unable to explain within their own frames of reference the reaction that our plays elicited. They were completely baffled by the hold that Toby had on his auditors.

"But the plot is so simple!" one of them said. "I just can't understand the audience getting such a thrill out of it."

He reminded me of a young fellow for whom Caroline and I once auditioned a comedy routine at NBC in Chicago. When we had finished, he practically dismissed us by saying, "Your dialect is wrong."

"Young man," I said, "you can tell me I'm that my material is bad and you're probably right. You can tell me I'm no comedian and you may be right. But when you talk about dialect you are dead wrong. I was born between those rows of corn and that's the only way I can talk."

Following several Florida winters in our trailer, we bought a home in Sarasota in 1951. I acquired a cruiser, joined the local power squadron, taught piloting and spent every available day out in the gulf chasing kingfish, mackerel or whatever else was running. It was such a nice life that I began to dream of retiring when I reached sixty-five. Caroline and I had bought annuities and had made some other investments with this in mind but as the time approached Caroline began to have other ideas. She talked often about how great the show still was going, what a shame it would be to close it and so on, so—as usual—we reached a compromise. While I continued to write the plays and direct, I retired altogether from the management and took no salary. It was a great arrangement. I kept doing everything that was fun to do and avoided all the work. Jay Bee Flesner was Caroline's manager for a couple of seasons and when he left the show Erman Gray took over. Erman came from an old tent show family—the Musical Grays, who once trouped in Missouri—and had been with us for several years, handling the orchestra and doing character parts.

Following the leisurely summer of 1957, I had a perfectly delightful winter in Sarasota, working only enough to assure The Schaffner Players a repertoire for the 1958 season. In March, as I was nearing the end of my writing, a long distance call came from George Eells, the theater editor of *Look,* who had visited our show several times and had become a good friend. He said some people out in Hollywood were going to make a movie called *Cavalcade of American Theater*, which would have a segment devoted to midwestern tent shows, and the producers wanted Caroline and me to come out, at their expense, for an audition. I complained that this was very difficult for us because we were getting ready for the new season but he insisted and I finally agreed to make the trip on the theory that it would be good for the show. There had been a lot of wonderful publicity *about* us, but here was a chance for the Schaffners to be *in* something. Actually what was happening was that Ralph Edwards was working on a "This Is Your Life" show about me and my career. Several people, including Caroline, had to be cut in on the secret and I must say they all did a perfectly magnificent job of deceiving me. Caroline turned out to be a wonderful liar—a talent I did not know about until then.

There were several times that I should have smelled a mouse —when they put us up in simply elegant quarters at the Sheraton Town House, for example, and when Eells called and said he and a representative of the producer would call on me at the hotel. In Hollywood, as everybody knows, you go to the producer's office and try to get in, but I was so preoccupied with the skit that I was writing for Caroline and me to do at the audition that I did not tumble. The day following our arrival, Eells showed up with a man he introduced as Dick Gordon, whose real name I later learned was Dick Gottlieb. He was Ralph Edwards's director. Gordon/Gottlieb asked all kinds of questions about repertoire, about Toby and about my career, and this continued for three days as he and Eells mysteriously herded me from studio to studio where movies were being made. In the meantime, Caroline always was somewhere else but she explained that while I was going through the interview routine they were keeping her busy at the costumers. At last, time came for the audition and Caroline left the hotel early under some pretext. Gordon/Gottlieb came for me in his own car and took me on a circuitous ride about Hollywood, pointing out places of interest which at the moment held no possible interest for me. When finally we reached the place where the audition was to be, I was ushered down a long hall with dressing rooms on either side. At last we came to an open door and there was Caroline, not in costume but in a new cocktail dress. I asked her what was going on and she said this was just a rehearsal for lights and such and she did not need to get into costume. Someone led me to the costume department, however, and there I picked out a suit that was the nearest thing to a Toby costume I could find; then we went to a room where there were a bunch of barber chairs and a young man waiting to do my makeup.

"Just give me the greasepaint and I'll put on the makeup," I said. "You wouldn't have any idea how to make up a Toby."

I made myself up, got into my costume and was about to glue my red wig down with spirit gum, as I always did, when Gordon/Gottlieb said, "Don't bother to glue it down, Neil—this is just a rehearsal and you won't need it that long." Another chap then led me down a hall to a place I presumed to be a movie set. We stopped behind some scenery and, out of habit, I peeked around and saw a number of people. The young man said it was customary in Hollywood to bring a few people in off the street to give the producers some idea of the public's reaction. I did not worry about *that*. (I learned later that there were more than eight hundred people but the lights were so arranged that I saw only the first row.) I kept running over the skit in my mind and after a while the young fellow put on some earphones and told me that when the time came for me to go on he would give me a little push. I then was to step on the stage and go into the mono-logue that led into our act. He gave me a push and I walked out on the stage and started in on some of my gags. Since this was only a rehearsal for lights, I did not try to put them over or any-thing like that—I just more or less jabbered to kill time. Out at the fringe of the lights a familiar face caught my eye. It was Bert Dexter, who had worked for us several years. That did not particularly surprise me because Bert had spent the previous winter in California, but I was puzzled momentarily by the box under his arm. He seemed to be selling candy. Then Harry Hogan materialized out of the lights and said, "Do you remember me? I played piano for you thirty years ago." I thought Harry Hogan was dead and when he sat down at the piano and began to play I thought to myself, maybe I'm dead, too—it was a spooky feeling. Then Ralph Edwards rose up out in the audience and came up to me.

"Do you have any idea what's going on here?" he asked.

"I haven't the slightest idea," I said, and he said, "Well, you are on television coast to coast because tonight, Neil Schaffner, This Is Your Life!"

I made a conscious effort to wake up and really did not become sure of my surroundings until Caroline came on stage and I felt her. She was warm.

What followed probably was the most exciting single occasion of my entire life. Germaine Lynn, with whom I had played on the Spedden & Paige show in 1909, was there; and Steve and Florence Burton, who were on the Gordonier show; Mayor Herb Sanders and his wife from West Burlington; my cousin, Flossie Hayden, and a number of others. Then Edwards said, "Neil Schaffner, This is Your Life! You have brought sunshine and laughter to millions. May your great gifts be with us for another thirty years!" The show was over. They took Caroline and me over to the Hollywood Roosevelt Hotel for an elaborate after-the-show party and there they turned up my old vaudeville partner, Bert Rose, and Milburn Stone and Kathy Nolan and Delores Dorn and a great many others whom we had known in repertoire over the years. The phone began to ring and telegrams poured in from all over the country bringing messages from old-timers in rep and others we had not heard from in ages.

4

Reaction to the Edwards show came quickly. The very next day, while I was out at Rome's house, Johnny Goetz of NBC called from New York to say that "Wide Wide World," the television show that Dave Garroway then was emceeing, was going to do a television program called "The Sound of Laughter," devoted to comedians of all kinds and types. They wanted us to appear. Goetz urged us to come into New York for a conference but we could not do that and so he met us back in Sarasota to work out the details. We opened at Washington, Iowa, and NBC erected three microwave towers on the lot to beam the picture to Des Moines, where it was fed into the network. It was a live show. Steve Allen did the opening segment in New York, then they jumped to Hollywood for a sketch with Bob Hope, and after that picked us up in Washington, doing a scene from one of our Toby plays. In his introduction, Garroway said, "Along the Mississippi, the sweet sound of laughter comes out of a tent. It's Toby in there getting the yocks—Neil Schaffner, the number one comedian of the nation's number one tent show."

Caroline got out window cards and handbills advertising "Toby & Susie—Stars of Omnibus, This Is Your Life and Wide Wide World." The show did fine business all through the summer, but a strange thing happened. We were not greeted, personally, with the same old warmth in some of our towns. This surprised and bothered me, especially in some of the towns where I really had expected the red carpet to be rolled out for us. I mentioned this one day to C. B. DePuy, the managing editor of the paper in Centerville.

"I'll tell you, Neil," he said, "when you were just a tent show man a lot of these people probably felt real democratic fraternizing with you. They felt superior and so they could afford to unbend. Now you have become a national figure. They no longer feel superior and they resent it."

At the end of the season we returned to Sarasota and things went wonderfully for us until February 1961 when I had a severe heart attack. Taking the show out for the summer was impossible, of course, so we stayed in Sarasota until the first of June, then went up to Wapello and parked the trailer on our lot overlooking the Iowa River, and I took it real easy all through the summer. Somewhere along the way I began to dream about a grand farewell tour. I mentioned it to Caroline and she seemed to like the idea.

One morning early in September I went up to the grocery store and a woman came up to me, beaming, and said, "Say, I saw you on television last night."

"You didn't see me," I said. "I was at home."

"I saw you all right," she said, "You and Susie."

I went over to the post office and someone there said they also had seen Toby and Susie on television but they were a little vague about the circumstances. I began checking around and found that NBC had broadcast a show called "Laughter U.S.A." on the "DuPont Show of the Week" and that it had, indeed, included some scenes from our show. I wrote Donald Hyatt, the producer, and asked if I might get a film clip of our part and he generously sent me a 16 mm. print of the whole show. It had film clips of the Keystone Cops, Charlie Chaplin, the Marx Brothers, Laurel and Hardy, Will Rogers and a number of other comedians over the years. George Burns did a fine and sensitive job as master of ceremonies. He spoke about the rube comedians from the days of George Washington, singling out Will Rogers as probably the outstanding one of them all. Then he said this kind of comedy still was going strong out in the Middle West. They showed some shots of our trucks going down the road and included an excerpt from one of our plays—

film that had been taken originally by Paul Feigay for "Omnibus."

"Nowadays they call him Toby," said Burns, "but it is the same simple, earthy humor that Abraham Lincoln was enjoying that night at Ford's Theater."

That did it. I began talking earnestly to Caroline about going out just one more time and then calling it quits. She was enthusiastic about going out again but not at all pleased about my idea of making it a farewell tour. She preferred to be in a position to go out still another year if the 1962 season did not prove too much of a strain for me. I argued that we might as well make up our minds to retire sometime and that this would be the way to do it—to go out in a blaze of glory—and ultimately she agreed there was logic to that. Working at a leisurely pace, I spent most of the winter in Sarasota preparing a repertoire of six plays for the tour. (We decided not to play Sundays.) All of the plays were comedies because this time, for sure, I wanted to leave them laughing.

Jimmy Davis, an Iowa boy who had been our leading man a couple of seasons before going into the Army, then was in Europe but was due to be coming home in time to join us on the tour. Since he was so well known all over our territory, I rewrote *The Girl Next Door*, working in many of the experiences in Europe that Jimmy had written us about, including the fact that he had won an all-Europe contest among Army entertainers. I called it *Back from Berlin*. Then I took the funniest scenes from several of our hillbilly shows and built a plot around superstitions of the hill people, calling it *Crystal Pool*. For the balance of the rep I did minor touch-up jobs on *Meet Dallas Daisie, Toby Goes to Washington, Mr. Wimple Has a Dimple* and *Stump Holler Folks*—each a different type and each a winner for us at various times over the years.

Caroline and I drove up to Wapello as usual in the latter part of April and began to organize the show. Preparations went along about as they always had, but as we started rehearsals I began to have some uneasy second thoughts about the tour. We had missed one whole season and my heart attack had been widely publicized. I began to wonder whether people still would think I was funny or would just pity me, and whether I had the stamina to give them the kind of a performance they had a right to expect. What would the year's layoff do to our business? As we wound up our rehearsals I just did not know what to expect. We opened on May 24, 1962—my seventieth birthday—to a large crowd and the show moved along just as it always had. Jimmy Davis read the advertising commercials from the mike backstage and the orchestra put on its usual concert and then I went out to make my customary opening talk. They laughed, and in all the right places. The first act went fairly well, though not as smoothly as I would have liked, but when the curtain dropped our schedule suddenly became a shambles.

E. A. Hicklen, a Wapello attorney, came up on the stage and someone who was in on the plot raised the curtain. Hicklen called Caroline and me out from the wings, made a graceful talk about our many years of close association with the town of Wapello and presented us with a beautifully framed citation bearing the official seal of the state of Iowa and signed by the governor, Norman A. Erbe. It said in part that "the people of Iowa will be forever grateful to Toby and Susie for their wonderful years of clean, wholesome entertainment." Then the sidewall of the tent was raised and the Wapello High School Band marched in, played a number, and swung into "Happy Birthday." The audience joined in singing. While this was going on, another sidewall was raised and Jim Hodge, the publisher of the local paper, and two or three other men brought in the largest birthday cake I ever saw. Dean Landfear, the program director of Station WMT in Cedar Rapids, came on and made an eloquent talk about our years in radio and presented us with a record and a booklet that described the stars who had appeared on the station over the years, including our pictures and excerpts from "Toby's Corntussle News."

It seemed entirely logical that Wapello would have made a little fuss over us since that was our summer home but I did not expect anything like that in any of the other towns. I would have been completely happy if they had just come to the show, in goodly numbers, and let me say goodbye and thanks in my own way. But every one of our towns heaped honors upon us and in many wonderful ways thanked *us* for what we had brought to them over the years. At Mt. Pleasant and Delta and Quincy, we were presented with beautifully inscribed citations and in Unionville, Edina and Lewistown, we received elaborate engraved plaques. At New Sharon, the chamber of commerce presented us with a heavy, engraved brass tray and in Kahoka, the city officials and the chamber of commerce gave us a beautiful silver tray. At Bloomfield, Iowa, the junior chamber of commerce presented us with their coveted Spark Plug Award, which is intended to recognize the local citizen who had been the "spark plug of the community" during the previous year. They told us it never had been presented before to an outsider. The cities of Quincy and Macon gave us keys to the city and in Kahoka the mayor said this really was unnecessary because "Toby and Susie already have the key to the hearts and minds of Kahoka and Clark County." Quincy College, a Catholic institution, made me an honorary trustee, gave us a citation praising our clean entertainment and presented Caroline with an immense bouquet of roses. At Vandalia and Centralia, the Odd Fellows Lodge, which had sponsored our appearances in those towns for many years, brought their highest state officer to the stage to make an address and present us with citations. In Centralia, Missouri's governor, John M. Dalton, also came on the stage to present us with a special award on behalf of my old and dear friend, L. Mitchell White, publisher of the *Mexico Ledger,* and his son Robert.

In Mt. Pleasant the ceremonies took place between the second and third acts of the play on opening night. I had a quick change to make for the third act and as soon as I could do so tastefully I ducked off the stage. I had just stripped down to my underwear and was reaching for my new costume when Bert Dexter ran up to the door of the dressing room and said, "Neil, get back out on that stage!"

Just then I heard a thunder of applause and asked Bert what was happening.

"They are giving you a standing ovation," he said.

Never in my life had I received a standing ovation and the only one I ever saw in the theater was given John Barrymore one night toward the end of his career. But there I was—caught with my pants off—and I could not even acknowledge it.

At New Sharon, where we always had set up our tent on the school grounds, a former president of the school board came on our stage on Saturday night and said he wanted to ask the audience to assist him in something. "I want you to imagine we are not here in the tent tonight but lined up along the sidewalks tomorrow morning when Toby and Susie are leaving our community," he said. "I'd like to have you join me in singing, 'God Be with You Till We Meet Again.' "

During the afternoon of opening day in New Sharon a pretty little girl came over to the tent and as she looked up at me tears started falling.

"My mother died of cancer just a short time ago," she said, "and one of the last things she said to me was, 'When Toby and Susie come, I want you to be sure and tell them how much I enjoyed their plays.' "

We never had gone through a season with fewer troubles. Weather was ideal for the most part and everywhere we played to huge crowds. We closed at Macon. On Saturday night the cast put on a special skit in our honor and presented us with a beautiful barometer bearing a brass plate on which all their names were inscribed. As we always had done on the last night of our season, we asked the audience to join us in singing "Auld Lang Syne." Tom Briggs, the president of the Lions Club made a touching speech about the "tremendous void" our departure would leave in Macon and at that point Caroline and I, too, were feeling a void of our own. But we were not yet through with tent rep. It had been our custom on the last night of the season to take out the insides of the tent and load them onto our trucks but to leave the tent standing until the next day so that it could dry out thoroughly before being stored for the winter. We barely had the trucks loaded that night when it began to rain. It rained all day Sunday and Sunday night and into Monday. The tent did not dry out until Wednesday.

As it turned out, we were not quite through with show business either. The week before our closing Dick Gottlieb called from Hollywood with an offer of a spot on a nationally televised show featuring Maurice Chevalier and we accepted it, thinking this would be a fine way to end our careers—or, just possibly, to start a new one on television. We wrote a skit based on a scene or two of *Toby Goes to Washington* and had a grand time doing the show. Reaction to our part was fine but no one came clamoring for our services, so after a visit of several days we went back to Iowa, packed our belongings and headed eastward for a long, leisurely cruise of the Mediterranean before settling down for the winter in Sarasota.

Fifty-five years, almost to the week, had passed since N. Edward Schaffner, The Original Silly Kid, made his first faltering steps toward becoming a professional entertainer. In all those years, there had been only two enforced absences—when Uncle Sam demanded my services in the First World War and in 1961 when the doctors forbade me to work. Forty-eight of those years were spent in repertoire.

In the eyes of many, repertoire was "small time," and from

the perspective of Broadway I suppose it was. Yet price is not the only criterion of value. I never saw a Broadway actor who could hold an audience the way Big Bill Bittner held it in *The Parish Priest*, nor any who measured up to Dick Henderson in *Dr. Jekyll and Mr. Hyde*, nor any of the famous Hamlets who were better than Hilliard Wight, who devoted the whole of his long career to small town opera houses. And in my time no comedian—on the stage, in the movies or on television—was funnier than Fred Wilson. Any theater that produces Laurette Taylor, Richard Bennett, Charles Winninger, Clark Gable, Warner Baxter, Lyle Talbot, Jennifer Jones, Milburn Stone, Delores Dorn and Irene Ryan needs no apologist and I am proud that I could be part of it for so long. In repertoire I saw more theater than most and—thanks to Cal Herman's durable creation, Toby —I was as big a headliner in my way as any of them.

Over the years Toby came in for much abuse from the self-anointed sophisticates of the theater, and the unknowing lumped the standard repertoire shows like The Schaffner Players with the gross and tawdry imitators that nipped around the edges of our territory and made the term "Toby show" an opprobrium. But the best of the Toby comedians were artists of a high order and I count it a privilege to have been among their number. I believe my own Toby was a credit to the theater and when I packed away the old red wig and wiped off the last freckles I felt that a part of me was gone forever.

I cannot even imagine these years having been different; certainly not the thirty-seven exhilarating and rewarding seasons with one of the hardiest troupers and finest comediennes of them all—my Caroline.

EPILOGUE

Here's Toby II

Here's Toby II

———————— ∼∼∼ ————————

THERE'S AN OLD SAYING AMONG TENT REPERTOIRE PEOPLE THAT the biggest boon to business is a rain before three o'clock in the afternoon—the theory being that farmers, chased out of the fields, become thoroughly bored at sitting around the house and, to escape, take their families to the show. Such an early afternoon rain one day in the early summer of 1952 proved to be an unusually big boon to The Schaffner Players. It not only brought the W. A. Davis family in to see the show but, very directly, contributed to the continuation of the Schaffner show beyond Toby and Susie.

Jimmie Davis at the time probably was the only fifteen-year-old boy in all of Louisa County, Iowa, who had never seen The Schaffner Players, and he would not have gone then if his mother had not caught him short. (On an earlier family excursion to the show, he had already made plans to go swimming with some of the other boys in the community and got off the hook.) Jimmie did not want to go; he expected to be thoroughly bored. Instead, he was enthralled. Among other things, he learned that every year the Schaffners held an amateur contest in their tent. Having already heard the sweet sound of applause in appearances before several school and church groups, playing one of the several musical instruments he had learned, Jimmie worked hard all winter devising an act for next summer's tent show. He had been tooting a trumpet ever since the third grade, when he first became a member of the school band. At about twelve he met a self-taught piano player who explained four basic chords to him and discovered that after several hours of concentrated practice he could play by ear any tune he could remember. Applying the same principle, he had taught himself the accordion and the guitar but for The Schaffner Players' amateur contest at Wapello in May 1953 he chose the piano—giving a very athletic, if not too tuneful, rendition with his hands in boxing gloves. He won so handily that he followed the show from town to town as long as it was within reach of the Davis farm, winning each contest (and three dollars cash) as handily as the first. Along the way he embellished the act considerably—ultimately doing it blindfolded with a blanket draped over the piano keys.

Audience response was so great and the actors on the Schaffner show, including Toby and Susie, were so friendly that Jimmie assumed getting a job on the show when it started out in the spring of 1955 would be easy. Unfortunately, the Schaffners had a rule that their people had to be at least eighteen; Jimmie was only seventeen. But, having decided that the tent show business was where he wanted to be, Jimmie went over to another Iowa tent show, the Sun Players, and talked himself aboard. He played curtain music on the piano, entertained in the nightly concert and otherwise made himself as useful as he could around the tent that summer and the next spring as he approached his eighteenth birthday, he plotted a scheme to get on The Schaffner Players for sure. The first step was to snag the light comedy lead in *Tell It to Tommy*, the 1955 senior class play at Wyman High School; the second was to invite Neil and Caroline Schaffner and other members of their then-assembling company out to see the performance.

"I was terribly nervous with them in the audience," Jimmie recalled, "but I did the very best I could and after the play they told me I had a job."

If the truth were known, the Schaffners probably already had decided to take Jimmie on, but Neil maintains the fiction that this performance had something to do with it. "Jimmie seemed to know more than anyone else what he was doing," says Neil.

During the summer Jimmie performed in the orchestra, did between-act specialties and played a few minor parts; in 1956 he graduated to a full line of leads. After the first season with the Schaffners, Jimmie enrolled at Iowa Wesleyan College at Mt. Pleasant, fully intending to get a college education between summer stints on the tent show, but this plan fell by the wayside after the 1956 season when Jay Bee Flesner, the Schaffners' character man and stage manager, suggested that Jimmie team up with him for a winter school tour. Between September and May they gave some two hundred shows before elementary and high school assembly audiences across the Middle West—Jay Bee reading poems and doing magic tricks and Jimmie providing the background music, singing a few songs and doing the boxing gloves bit on the piano. When tent show season rolled around again, Flesner returned to The Schaffner Players but, concluding that "two years on one show was enough for the public," Jimmie signed on with the Collier Players, a small family show in Illinois. The Colliers closed earlier than the Schaffners so he rejoined Toby and Susie in mid-September, selling advertising banners, working the orchestra and doing specialties until their season ended. He never left them again, though Uncle Sam did enforce one two-year furlough in 1960-61.

The Army trained Jimmie as a radio operator and sent him to Germany. There he discovered the All-Army Entertainment Contest, in which he placed first in Europe and third in the international competition in Washington—with the boxing gloves and blanket act, naturally. This led to a European tour, as a whistler, with the United States Air Force Band during which he figures he played to eighty million people, in concert and on radio, on both sides of the Iron Curtain, and this, in turn, led

to a six-month tour with his own one-man show. After entertaining American and other Allied troops at missile bases and
other installations in the United Kingdom, Italy, France, Switz-
erland, Belgium and Germany, the Army asked him to perform
for troops of the German army as well. Fortunately, during his
first couple of months in Germany Jimmie had applied himself
seriously and had picked up a conversational knowledge of the
language, and his corn-country jokes went over as big with the
Germans as they had with the Americans.

"Finding out that I could make people laugh while telling
jokes in their language," says Jimmie, "was the most rewarding
experience of all."

All of this came to an end, fortunately, in time for Jimmie to
join the Schaffners for their triumphant farewell tour. Return
to the show also made it possible for him to get on with another
major project.

After completing his basic training in 1959, Jimmie had been
given a short leave and after visiting his family in Louisa County
he naturally went over to see the Schaffners. There he found
that the new ingenue was a beautiful little brunette from Men-
don, Illinois who, like Jimmie, had won several Schaffner amateur contests and, on turning eighteen, had joined the show. Her
name was Juanita Bellomy.

"I remembered her," Jimmie recalled later. "She won the 1955
contest at Quincy with a saxophone solo, and it was pretty good,
but she was just thirteen and I was eighteen and not much interested in girls of that age. When I saw her again in 1960 I was
surprised to find out how much she had grown, and how nicely.
We had a date or two before I left for Germany and I wrote her
all the time I was in the service. When I went back on The
Schaffner Players in 1962, she was working in Quincy. I couldn't
leave the show so she courted me all summer. We never were
more than two hundred miles from her home but during the
summer she drove twelve thousand miles so that we could be

together on weekends. When the show closed in September we
got married and started right out on a school tour together. We
have been playing schools in winter and the tent in summer
ever since."

When rehearsals for the farewell tour began, Jimmie raised
the question of taking the show out himself after the Schaffners'
retirement and although no deal actually was made Neil decided
to test the public pulse by giving Jimmie the Toby part, sans
wig, in the Saturday night bill, *Meet Dallas Daisie*.

"All through the summer, Neil kept dropping hints that something was in the wind," Jimmie said. "He gave me a little extra
buildup in his nightly talks before the opening curtain and although to avoid confusion—because Neil was doing five other
Tobies on the week—we did not call my part Toby on Saturday
night, I think most people in our audiences recognized they were
getting a preview of what was to come. As civic leaders began
to shower Neil and Caroline with honors I more or less took over
the ceremonies and so the public got accustomed to me doing
most of the things that Neil usually did."

When the season ended, Caroline offered Jimmie a partnership
—much as J. S. Angell had made Neil his partner back in 1924—
and both she and Neil trouped with the show throughout the
1963 season. (Neil directed and Caroline took up tickets.) On
opening night in each town, Neil introduced Jimmie as "Tobias
T. Tolliver the Second" and presented him with a red wig.

"Jimmie, when I created the character of Toby I wanted
something distinctive—something in the manner of a uniform—
and what I hit upon was this old red wig," he said. "I want you
to wear it with pride and honor. If you give these people the
same kind of clean, wholesome entertainment that Toby always
brought them, I am sure you will be able to carry on for thirty
more years."

Toby II turned out to be pretty much a carbon copy of the character the patrons of The Schaffner Players had come to know and love—even to the ad libs—and the show did so well that summer that Jimmie and Juanita bought it outright the following winter. Neil and Caroline agreed that they could continue calling the show The Schaffner Players and their 1964 advertising hailed the extension of "a living legend in the Midwest."

1963—Rebirth of a Tradition—1963

AMERICA'S ONLY FOLK THEATER

The Internationally Famous

SCHAFFNER PLAYERS

Created by the Legendary

TOBY AND SUSIE

Now Starring the Young and Brilliant Comedian

JIMMIE DAVIS

In the Tent Theater Beautiful

As Juanita became better known, the billing changed but the theme remained the same. In 1967 it said:

James and Juanita Davis Present

The 42nd Annual Tour of the

Internationally Famous ...

SCHAFFNER PLAYERS

As created by the Legendary

TOBY AND SUSIE

Other parts of the announcement declared: "Here's Toby! ... as portrayed by the versatile and talented Jimmie Davis ... Co-starring Illinois's loveliest daughter, Juanita Davis, appearing nightly in leading roles and director of The Schaffner Players' New Vaudeville Band."

The format remained essentially the same as it had been for years, with one exception. Susie was missing.

"Toby and Susie have retired," says Jimmie. "There must be a Toby—what would The Schaffner Players be without him?— but the Toby and Susie team belongs forever with Neil and Caroline. When we use a Schaffner play we change the name of the Susie character and Juanita never plays it. She someday may move from leads to characters but I doubt that she ever will play a part quite like Susie."

Other, more subtle changes were beginning to manifest themselves as Jimmie and Juanita began their fourth season, in 1967, as owners and managers of the show. Four members of the cast were college students—chosen from among more than fifty auditioned under the sponsorship of the heads of drama departments at the universities of Iowa, Illinois and Missouri.

"No other tent show ever managed *that*," Neil Schaffner observed.

Talks were under way, also, about taking the show to the University of Iowa campus in 1968, and perhaps to other universities later on. Jimmie was talking guardedly about the possibility of presenting a musical. Meanwhile, he was addressing himself to a number of interesting physical changes. Dressing rooms backstage, for example, had hot and cold running water— something unheard-of before around tent shows—and built-in closets and lockers had replaced the traditional actors' wardrobe trunks. Out front, the blues were gone. Everybody had a "soft pine chair" to sit upon for a single price at the front door (eighty-five cents for adults and sixty cents for children in most places, but never more than a dollar). Harking back to the days when most tent shows advertised themselves with a "marching band" parade downtown, the ten-piece Schaffner Players' New Vaudeville Band made a daily ballyhoo swing around town, riding in a specially-built trailer drawn by a sparkling new Chevrolet van with a built-in amplifying system.

Already there had been numerous tempting offers to set up the tent at resort areas near large midwestern cities for an entire season of summer stock, but the Davises refused even to consider such a thing.

"The Schaffner Players has a long and proud tradition," says Jimmie. "The show has been on the road longer than any other in the history of tent repertoire and soon it will be the only one left. We want it to go on and on as it is—up and down those rows of corn."

Jimmie and Juanita evidently are planning for the long range. On Friday night of the 1967 opening week in Wapello, Brant Alan Davis, age twenty-one months, made his tent rep debut with a hearty solo turn between acts on the drums.

VANCE JOHNSON

INDEX